Theresa A. Fersch

Returning from the Camino

Lessons from a Life-Changing Journey

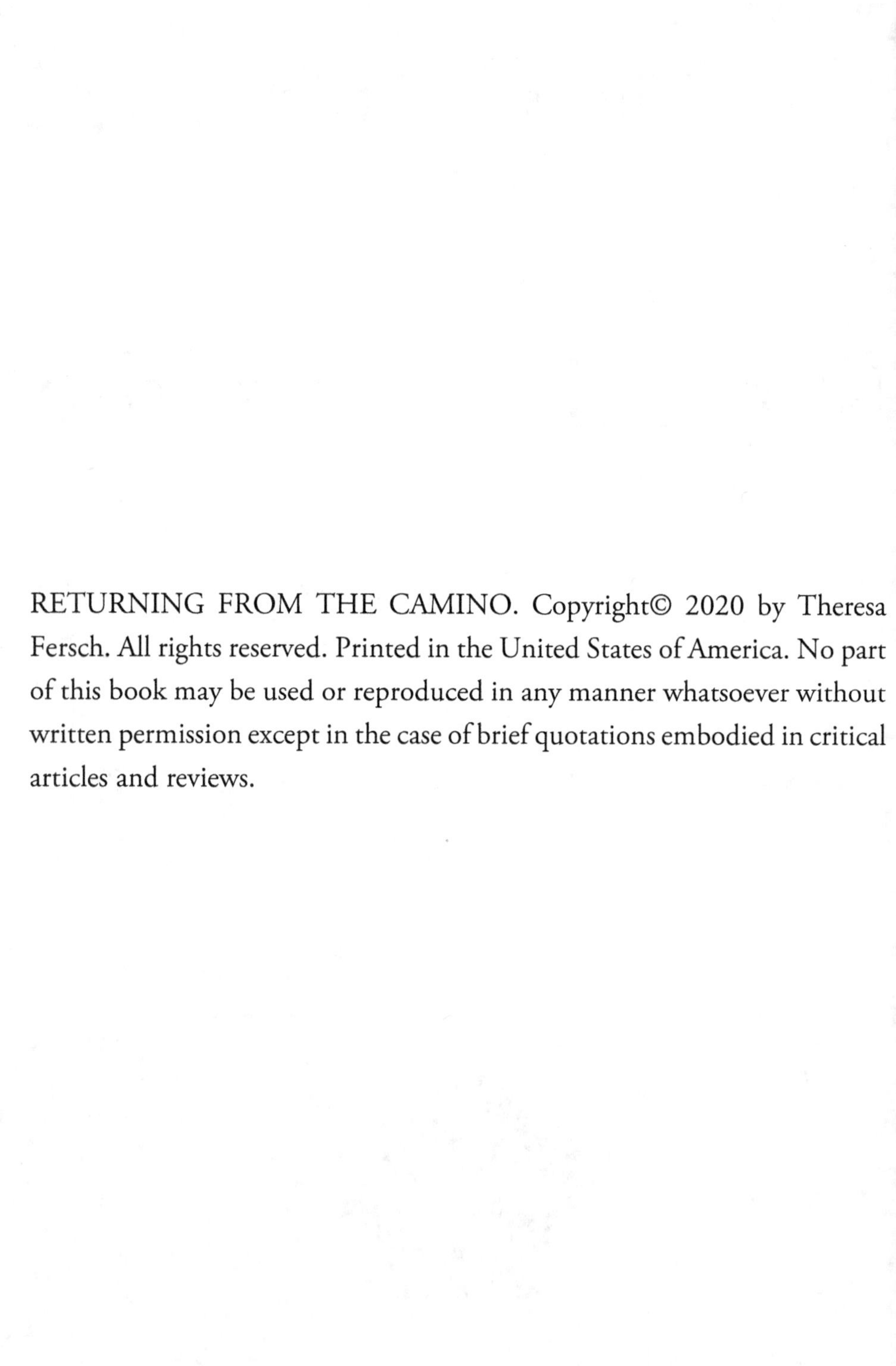

Contents

PREFACE

Five years ago, I arrived at the front steps of the cathedral in Santiago de Compostela, Spain. I hiked nearly five hundred miles, from St. Jean Pied de Port, France, over the Pyrenees Mountains, and across Spain, the most majestic country I've had the privilege of knowing. I frolicked in wheat fields, slept in castles, and dined in unique restaurants. I prayed in ancient cathedrals, napped in sprawling poppy fields, and walked through miles of vineyards. I drank superb wine, made lifelong friends, and gained unforgettable memories.

While on pilgrimage, I experienced a spectrum of events and emotions that I never thought possible. I laughed, I cried, I felt like a Rockstar, and I felt utterly vulnerable. I began as a reluctant and naive but optimistic young woman, and finished as an accomplished, experienced, and grateful pilgrim. In the 38 days it took me to reach Santiago, I danced in the intangible gifts of a life-changing journey and experienced a lifetime of lessons.

When I arrived, I gazed up at that magnificent cathedral and soaked in feelings of satisfaction, pride, gratitude, and faith. *Wow, this is what it feels like to accomplish something amazing.* But what does it all mean? What happens now?

What I didn't know in that moment was that the end of my Camino was just the beginning of my journey. The pilgrimage bestowed onto me life lessons and gifts that took me years to unpack and process.

We all change as time goes on. We adapt to the world around us as life events inspire us in different ways. But what I have come to learn is that some life events shock our core, awaken our spirit, and have the power to completely alter the course of our life. Hiking the Camino de Santiago in 2015 did exactly that for me. I prepared myself to embark on a new adventure with excitement and cautiousness and I had the time of my life.

That said, the true work, the transformation, did not begin until I returned home. Over the last five years, my life has morphed and shaped itself in the most wonderful and painful ways. The Camino triggered a sequence of events and launched me into a life I never could have imagined for myself without having taken that first leap of faith to do something amazing. I am now a world traveler, an adventurer, an athlete, a public speaker, an author, and a number of other things I never would have pegged myself for.

Many people read about the adventures of the Camino de Santiago seeking wisdom and wonder, but I believe there is an even better story to be told about one's return from a long-distance hike, and I believe others need to hear the wonderful gifts that come with pushing yourself outside of your comfort zone. I want others to know that when they trust themselves and take small, calculated risks, they can find themselves happier, healthier, and living their life to the fullest extent.

The truth is, there was a time when I didn't fully understand why people push themselves to be "conquerors of the useless." When my husband would call me from the Appalachian Trail all bruised and battered, I'd ask myself "is life SO boring that people have to create unnecessary challenges for themselves?" But once I hiked the Camino, I realized the answer to that question is YES! Very few people in the modern industrialized world have the opportunity to experience something truly extraordinary. Few push themselves beyond any visible horizon to accomplish something amazing. But when you push yourself, when you dig deep down and you pull out all of your strength, courage, and conviction to accomplish a challenge put before you, you reach a level of self-awareness that is unattainable any other way. You discover all of your strengths and all of your weaknesses. You are met with yourself. There is no denying, there is no hiding, there is no lying about who you are and what you are capable of. This is why people push themselves to do incredible things. I found myself for the first time on the Camino and it is my wish for everyone to have such powerful experiences.

Just a Little Background

My husband, Brian, hiked the entire length of the 2,200-mile Appalachian Trail (AT) in 2014. When he returned, he was bursting with what I can only describe as his human spirit. He thoroughly enjoyed the trials and tribulations of his nearly seven-month journey and came back a stronger, better, and happier man. That said, he seemed to be going through something on a deep personal level, something that was not only difficult for him to articulate but also difficult for me to watch as an outsider. He was noticeably struggling to adjust to his former life. I didn't really understand, but I witnessed, somewhat helplessly, as he flailed in the beginning. I recognized that being away from all the hustle and bustle of modern-day life for long periods of time would most certainly have an impact on anyone, but that was the extent of my understanding. I didn't quite get what he had been through while on the trail either, but whatever happened, it was life altering. Despite his struggle and mild "trail depression," he found his way. He had a deeper love, gratitude, and respect for the world, and he was dedicated to being the best man, husband, son, and friend he could be. We grew closer and stronger than ever.

Brian told me, "Theresa, you have to do something amazing for yourself. You have to have your own adventure." He spoke loosely of the transformative nature of a long-distance hike and strongly encouraged me to find an adventure. The AT did not speak to me the way it did to Brian, so I sought out a similar experience that better suited me.

Deciding to hike the Camino de Santiago was a meandering

sequence of events that occurred over the course of several months. My introduction to the Camino was, in fact, less than inspiring. When Brian was hiking the southern portion of the Appalachian Trail, I flew down to Blacksburg, Virginia and visited him while he rested in town for a few days. We spent Easter weekend at a beautiful bed and breakfast in the college town, owned by a very hospitable couple.

Brian and I spent all day Saturday talking as we sat on the porch swing of the B&B. For the first time in our young marriage, we were having a fairly serious conflict. It seemed that while he was away having a grand time, all the small marital issues we normally managed easily came bubbling to the surface. With him being absent from our life at home, we were unable to address them before they became too serious. We sat on that swing for eight hours, hashing out our grievances and finding compromises. It was a complex but healing discussion that left us both feeling much better about our life together.

While we were sitting there, having this intense discussion, the friendly B&B owners came by and began talking to us. They were intrigued by Brian's ambitious endeavor and spoke excitedly of an amazing hike in Spain called the Camino de Santiago. They said the Camino pilgrims walk from town to town, indulging in Spanish food, wine, and culture. At the time, I acted interested because it felt like the polite thing to do, but honestly, I just wanted to return my attention to Brian. They had a copy of the movie *The Way,* which takes place on the Camino, and offered to let us borrow it so we could watch it. Feeling a bit cheeky, I said, "We haven't seen each other in two months. I didn't fly down here to watch movies." They had a good laugh and let us return to our conversation.

I didn't give it another thought until one evening months later, after Brian returned home, when he challenged me to expect more from my life. We were talking about taking a vacation together when the woman's words crept into the forefront of my mind. "What was the name of that hike she told us about?"

And so began our research. We learned that the Camino is a spiritual pilgrimage and people come from all over the world to give witness to the remains of St. James the Apostle, which lay in the famous cathedral in Santiago de Compostela. I was immediately drawn to Santiago. I loved that it was in a foreign country I had never previously considered visiting. It was also appealing because there was a solid infrastructure along the way with restaurants and places to sleep which means I would not have to camp or carry a lot of food. I also learned that about half the people who walk it are solo female hikers, and that many people walk it for spiritual reasons. Brian and I talked about how we should take two weeks off work to hike the last 60 miles of the Camino Frances, leading to Santiago, which is the "official" Camino. But I learned that many people begin their pilgrimage in St. Jean Pied de Port, a small town in France about 500 miles from Santiago. I began thinking about how transformed Brian was from his long-distance hike, and I suddenly felt compelled to push myself in a way that I never had before. "Should I do the entire Camino?" I asked as we were getting ready for bed. Without hesitation Brian said, "Yes, and you should do it alone. It'll change you." I stopped what I was doing to take in his words. They were powerful, inspiring, and I knew at that moment I was going to do it. That very night, I texted a friend and told her I was going to hike the Camino even before I knew much about it. To this day, I remember the sound of Brian's words and my sudden determination.

Of course, there was always an aching bit of doubt lurking in the pit of my stomach, but I worked hard to ignore it. When people would ask me if I was crazy, or what would possess me to do something so insane, or suggest that I was being immature, irresponsible, foolish, and even selfish for traveling by myself, that doubtful stomach ache would fester. *What exactly am I thinking? What makes me think that I of all people can do this? I've never done anything like this in my life!* But with each doubting moment, I remembered first that people said the same dreadful things to Brian when he planned to hike the AT. Then I remembered Brian's words: "You have to do something amazing." So, I embraced his support, heeded his advice, dismissed the doubters, and crushed that doubt with contempt and determination. I was going to do this! I looked for inspiration wherever I could to fuel that positive energy. I found a meme with a female backpacker overlooking a vast mountain range with a caption that read, "Sometimes the fear won't go away, so you'll just have to do it afraid." I printed the image and taped it to the wall in my office months before I left for Europe.

And so it went. I did more research and planning, put a pack on my back, jumped on a plane, and next thing I knew I was on the Camino. Brian suggested I start a blog so other people could follow me through my adventure, so I created a simple website not intending to use it much. I maintained this blog through which I journaled my experiences as they played out. I had never blogged before and truth be told, the only reason I did was because I promised my mom I'd stay in touch every day and let her know I was still alive. I attempted to manage the expectations of my handful of interested readers by admitting my journaling would probably consist of merely a few drunken photos offered up as a proof-of-life. To my complete surprise, journaling at the end of each day became a critical part of my trail experience. I began to love the hours I spent every evening all to myself, documenting my thoughts and experiences as I embarked on the greatest challenge and foreign adventure of my life.

As I continued, my journaling became increasingly important to me. Not only did it force me to take time each day to reflect on my trip, but friends, family, and colleagues would leave encouraging comments which I was especially grateful for during the tough times.

When I returned home, I learned that I had hundreds of readers, most of whom I did not know. It seemed that while I only shared my website with a few special people, the link had spread like wildfire. I couldn't understand why anyone would want to know what I was doing. But I eventually came to realize that people are hungry for adventure, and what they crave most in this world of Instagram perfection and Facebook phoniness is honesty, vulnerability, and truth. My blog was bursting with all of that as I withheld nothing. I talked about all the wonderful experiences I had along the way: the food, the scenery, the people, the churches. But I also did not shy away from the tough, ugly parts of myself and my travels. I shared when I clumsily knocked myself in the face with my hiking pole, earning myself an instant goose egg. I shared when I had blisters that impeded my journey and I cried hopelessly in the shower. I wrote about how heartbroken I was when I had to say goodbye to friends. I openly expressed my cockiness when I felt newer pilgrims were interfering with "my Camino". I talked frankly about my serious doubts about finishing the trail, and I discussed the difficulties Brian and I experienced when he finally joined me for the last 100 miles of the Camino.

The benefits of diligently documenting these truths were twofold. First, I personally grew and matured as I captured every detail of my journey. Second, I learned that others were also benefiting from the opportunity to see the Camino, if only from afar, and witness one example of humanity in all its imperfection.

Once I converted my blog into a book, *Sunrise in Spain*, my story was disseminated more broadly than I could have ever imagined. While those around me lovingly encouraged me to publish my story, I honestly believed my mother would be the only one to read it. So, you can imagine my surprise when thousands of people read it within the first year! Right around that same time, I began giving talks about my Camino. My first talk was at the public library in my small New Hampshire hometown. It was well received and I began getting calls from all over the state. As I gave more talks, my presentation slowly morphed from a basic description of the Camino experience into a personal message to everyone who came to hear me speak, that they too should find out what drives them, that secret grand adventure they have always wanted to tackle but have never felt capable of doing. Soon, I found myself wanting to encourage strangers to reach for something amazing, to take risks, to work towards enhancing their life in ways they didn't dream were possible. Admittedly, I did so not fully understanding where that message was coming from inside me. After a few years, I had given my talk nearly 50 times in five states to audiences as small as three people and as large as 300.

In the meantime, I was receiving a fair amount of pressure to write another book. While *Sunrise in Spain* included a daily account of what I was experiencing, it had little to no reflection. In fact, of the critical comments I received from readers, one was that I didn't talk enough about what the journey meant to me. I came to realize that those who expected this of me had never had a life-changing adventure of their own. If they had, they would have understood that it is impossible to truly reflect on such a monumental experience while it's happening. The truth is, it took several years of processing for me to start understanding its meaning. But I also understood people's desire to know how a trip like that can impact someone. I made true attempts to begin writing within a year of coming home, but each time I started to write, I was left feeling strained and exhausted. My dear friend Jess, who helped make my first book possible, encouraged me to begin writing whatever came to mind just to see what would come from the exercise, a "brain dump." After focusing on the project for days I had a detailed account of the first few weeks following my return from the Camino, but the words were sad, foggy, and without purpose. The story was there, but it lacked meaning. I couldn't make sense of any of it. I just wasn't ready. I did however hang onto those details I captured, which I'm grateful for now, because even a year later I had forgotten many of those moments despite being critical milestones in my transformation.

As I continued to speak openly about my time in Spain and as I worked to improve my health and lifestyle over time, those lessons I gained from the Camino started to resonate with me. I would be in the middle of a presentation and suddenly have a realization about how the Camino had changed me. I would race home after the event and write down my thoughts. Soon, the realizations were becoming more cohesive and would overwhelm my concentration. The events of my life following the Camino were beginning to make sense and suddenly, one day several years later, I was inspired for my own reasons to put the pen to paper once again and continue documenting my journey. Unlike with my first book, which I wrote day-to-day while in Spain, this book was written in massive waves of inspiration and curiosity. I decided to ride those waves as they came to me with no expectations, and in doing so I am continuing to learn more about myself every day.

What I learned from working on this book though is that writing about the effects of the Camino is far more challenging than merely journaling the daily details of the experience itself. Reflection requires far more consideration, it requires brutal honesty, and I realized why many people have written about their time on the Camino but not about the lessons they gained from the trip years after. This book became far more personal than I ever imagined it should be, but I cannot provide an example of how the Camino changes someone without first describing how they were before the life-changing event.

I struggled with how revealing and personal my first book was, but this one is by far the most painfully revealing thing I've ever shared openly.

While I am bursting with inspiration, purpose, and am thrilled to be alive right now, I did not arrive at this amazing place easily. The return from the Camino was quite honestly crushing in the most unexpected ways; I struggled tremendously to get here and I know, God willing, this is only one of many more phases of my life. I feel I owe it to my readers to share my own personal experience in the hopes that it'll help them deal with their own which may or may not be similar to mine.

The Camino Actually
Begins in Santiago

One of the most fascinating aspects of a life-changing journey for me is the glacial pace it takes to process. I thought I walked slow on the Camino, but good Lord, processing it has taken even longer. Immediately following the Camino, my life was a complete blur however, it wasn't until a couple years later that I started to understand what any of it meant. I wasn't prepared for this process though and had unreasonable expectations for how long I thought I would need to find myself again. While most of *Sunrise in Spain* was written when I was on the Camino, the final chapter was my "six-month reflection". I'm laughing at myself as I write this because I remember how much I struggled with that chapter and secretly hated it because it felt so forced. The truth is, that reflection was almost completely fabricated, practically a lie, fueled by a confused, stressed pilgrim who felt pressure to find "closure" and conclude the book with a pretty ribbon. I felt that my readers deserved to have a happy ending. I wanted to be gifted with gratitude and clarity and to share that positivity with others. But the truth is, six months after my adventure, when I wrote that final chapter, I was still trying to make sense of the emotions and changes I was going through. I would eventually come to realize that the Camino is a life-long journey that begins in Santiago de Compostela and eventually I would come to accept its continuous nature. But six months after my trip, I was beating myself up for not "moving on" quickly enough.

Because I had all these amazing experiences on the Camino, when I returned home, I expected to come back a complete person: positive, confident, renewed, and insanely happy about the world. But the truth is my return was far from the fairytale I envisioned. Transformation is not pretty. It's painful and it's lonely.

When Brian returned home from the Appalachian Trail, he was very different in surprising ways. There were the more obvious but smaller changes; suddenly he wasn't accustomed to having a selection of clothes to choose from and he insisted on wearing the same shirt every day. By day four of his return, I had to reintroduce him to his closet and convince him to peel off the dirty shirt he had been sporting for the better part of a week. His driving skills had noticeably deteriorated over the months he'd been gone, and he could no longer sleep in our room unless there was an arctic breeze passing through continuously. But something deeper was going on, too. Brian is generally a happy guy, but after the trail there was a lingering sadness and longing in the air. He missed the trail; he missed his trail family. He struggled at work and by the time he came home he was so stressed about the day that there wasn't much left to be positive about. Eventually though he found peace with his life and he seemed to settle in quite nicely after a few months, though he admits to this day, over six years later, he still has to work to find balance in his life.

Now, here's the thing: I witnessed all of this. I saw the man I love go through changes, saw him struggle, and saw him recover to an even better state than before the AT. He had been gone for nearly seven months so naturally, I believed these were the consequence of being away from civilization for so long. Despite seeing this first hand, it never occurred to me that I would experience a similar upheaval as he did because my trip was a mere six weeks compared to his trip which took up the better part of a year…man, did I misjudge that one.

My First Week Home

Brian returned to work immediately following our trip to Spain. He had joined me for the very end of the Camino and had the opportunity to experience the last hundred miles of it with me. I was glad he did this overall because it gave him a taste of what I had been doing for over a month. Upon reaching Santiago, we took a bus to the coast to visit two towns, Finisterre and Muxia, and then spent several more days touring Madrid and Barcelona before coming home. So, while Brian did see some of the Camino, it was more of a standard vacation for him than the personal pilgrimage it had become for me. He returned to work and life as soon as we got back to New Hampshire. I, on the other hand, took an additional week off work to acclimate, as was recommended within the Camino community. I had read from numerous sources that it's important for a pilgrim to return slowly back to "real life." I didn't believe I would need the entire week to recover, and assumed after a few days I would become bored and would want to return to work, but I quickly learned that I needed much longer than a week.

Brian was already at work when I awoke that first morning at home, and it left me feeling lonely. I had become accustomed to sharing sleeping quarters with dozens of happy pilgrims and waking surrounded by loving friends. I missed the community. *Where are all my pilgrims?* I thought. I knew I was just adjusting to being alone again, so I looked for ways to ease the transition. I had also become accustomed to praying frequently on the Camino. Nothing too deep, but a continuous conversation with God throughout the day. *I'll just talk to God,* I thought. I tried as I had done many times on the Camino but now it felt different, empty. I wasn't getting a response. The comfort I felt from praying on the Camino was no longer abundantly available to me. I told myself the feeling would pass when I hung out with my friends later that week.

I spent the majority of my week at home, sifting through the 3,000 pictures and videos I took from the Camino, paring them down into an entertaining movie I could share with everyone. As I scrolled through those images, conjuring up memories from the best time of my life, I became acutely aware of this fogginess that began engulfing my brain. It felt as though critical thinking and decision making were still on vacation and had left me brainless. Suddenly, I couldn't even remember how to make simple decisions. It was as if I had to relearn how to do routine things again. I went from living a simple life on the Camino where all I did was eat, sleep, walk, and connect with others to suddenly being thrust into a world full of chores and decisions, all of which felt completely pointless and unfulfilling. Additionally, there was this lingering, deeply rooted sadness I could feel festering.

Consumed by Grief

One of the main sources of that sadness which I was able to identify was brought on by the death of my beautiful grandmother. Grandma Rose passed while I was still in Spain and I deeply regretted not being home to help. My mom was by her side, in her home, up until the very end, and I knew that with my hospice training I could have helped make both of them more comfortable in those final hours. Instead, I was gallivanting around Spain and missed the entire thing.

My mom called me the day after I returned home and informed me that the funeral was in two days. The moment she told me, I knew deep in my gut there was no way I could make it. I was struggling just to function between the jetlag and the sudden unexplainable cloudiness I was experiencing. I knew the ten-hour drive to Ohio, where my grandma would be buried, would be extremely difficult, and Brian wouldn't even be able to accompany me because he used all his vacation time in Spain. *Theresa, you won't make it to Ohio.* I had images of someone informing my mother at her own mother's funeral that her daughter was killed in an accident after falling asleep behind the wheel. I couldn't do it. "Mom...I'm not going to be able to make it." I held my breath.

Her response was short but teeming with emotion. "Are you serious?" She was utterly shocked. Her barely audible words sounded as though I had slapped her across the face and left no energy in her body. Her disbelief and devastation were heart wrenching. I said I was so sorry but there was nothing more I could say or do. I couldn't explain what I was going through and I knew at that moment she was in no condition to hear about my problems. I knew she'd be disappointed in me for a long time, and there wasn't a thing I could do about it. I apologized once again and we hung up.

On the day of my grandmother's funeral, I sat on my living room couch, staring at the light patterns on the carpet and watched them slowly shift over the hours as the sun crossed the sky and passed through the windows. I didn't move once, paralyzed with grief, guilt, and a sense of Camino depression. I received several angry calls that day from irate relatives who honestly couldn't believe I wasn't attending the funeral. My tone was emotionless and flat as I told them I could not come, which made them even angrier. By the third phone call, I let it go to voicemail. I couldn't bear again telling someone I wasn't going without having an explanation I could articulate. It was one of the worst days of my life.

Reconnecting with Friends

I knew the damage I had done to my family on the day of my grandmother's funeral would require careful attention and healing but it wasn't something I could manage just yet. That evening, Brian and I got together for dinner with two of our good friends, Matt and Liz. I was so excited to see them after all this time and to interact with people in a fun way. We arrived at our favorite Korean restaurant and ordered stiff drinks. "So how was the Camino?!" Liz asked in her usual bubbly and excited style. I opened my mouth to respond and realized I didn't know what to say. How could I possibly sum up my entire experience to them? How could I answer that question? How could I share with them every amazing and painful event that has led me to this point in my life? I was aware that somehow I was different now but couldn't explain why or how. I suddenly realized that no matter what I chose to say, there was no way I could make them understand what my trip meant to me. They wouldn't know what I experienced and, oh my God...*they don't even know who I am anymore.* The innocent and well-intentioned question left me feeling utterly alone and with that loneliness came a wave of depression like I've never felt before.

All these thoughts and emotions flickered through me in the blink of an eye. I tried to recover quickly, pulled on a fake smile and said, "It was awesome." I hastily conjured up some stories from the Camino that I thought would be fun and compelling, offering evidence of how happy I should have been feeling. I'm not sure if they believed my facade but they happily went along with the stories, chiming in with appropriately timed "ooohs" and "aahhs."

As Brian and I drove home that night, I sat quietly looking out the window trying to understand why I suddenly felt so disconnected from myself and my loved ones. *Theresa, what is wrong with you?*

Returning to Work

The following Monday I returned to work with enthusiasm. I was looking forward to seeing my colleagues again and I knew they'd have lots of questions about my adventure because many of them read my blog and left encouraging comments. The previous week was rough but I was eager to jump back into my life carrying with me all the positive energy I harnessed from the Camino.

I spoke in my last book of the restlessness I experienced my first day home. Try to imagine the physical adjustment that must be made after a long-distance hike. Just as suddenly walking 20 miles a day is very hard on your body, so is suddenly not walking 20 miles a day. I went from being outside under the sun, all day, every day, exerting myself, to sitting in a room with no windows eight hours a day. It was extremely difficult on my mind and body. The first thing I noticed upon returning to work was the perpetual need to move forward at all times. Every 10 minutes, I would stand up and walk out of my office but didn't have anywhere to go. I refilled my water bottle repeatedly and visited the bathroom more times than I needed.

On the Camino, I had a goal each day, I had purpose. I picked a spot on a map and I endeavored all day to reach that goal. Every day, when I arrived at my destination, I felt like I accomplished something major. I felt like a Rockstar. When I returned home, I no longer had a daily goal. I stepped through those first few days at work moment by moment, trying to find essential goals, but suddenly, my life had no purpose, no meaning. This may be difficult to understand, but there were two diametrically opposing parts of me when I returned to my life back home. The first was an eager, excited, rejuvenated Theresa who loved everyone and was completely grateful for the spiritual trip she just experienced. But there was also this second layer that loomed overhead, threatening to take over every moment of my day. This second part was a latently sad, lonely, and "fuzzy" Theresa who could barely function. I desperately tried to embrace the first Theresa. When I returned to work, everyone was very happy to see me and welcomed me back with a kindness I had become accustomed to on the Camino. *I can do this,* I told myself. I shared my favorite stories with lots of gesturing and my notorious booming laughter. It felt so good to relive those amazing moments of my life. If I was talking about the Camino, I felt great. But as soon as matters shifted, or as soon as it got quiet, this second Theresa would rear its ugly head. I didn't want to appear ungrateful for everything I had been through, and I wanted so much to feel as happy and as free as I did on the Camino so I did everything I could to keep my spirits high. I smiled big, laughed hard, and guzzled coffee, which I had developed a mild addiction to while in Spain.

My officemate of eight years was so happy and relieved to have me back in the office and safely within view. She followed my blog like a nervous mother and welcomed me back wholeheartedly. It was so good to see her again, as I missed her friendship, but like with my other friends, I felt this barricade between us. I could talk until I was blue in the face, but she wouldn't know how I'd changed. Not that I could expect her to since I didn't even know. Usually after going on vacation or being away from each other for a while we would spend a good deal of time catching up. I did spend some time elaborating on the stories she was familiar with from my blog, all the while feeling alienated. I believe I successfully hid this dark part of me from everyone else at work, but after knowing me for so many years, my officemate was not fooled. She knew something was wrong and told me much later that she could feel the sudden "distance" between us.

I was sitting at my desk that first morning back, reading through hundreds of emails and trying to figure out what was wrong with me and how I was going to move on despite the collision going on in my head. An instant message popped up on my screen from my friend and colleague, Tom. "Welcome back. Are you ready to work?" My stomach did a somersault. *I'm so not ready for this.* "Yes!" I replied. I decided I would fake it for as long as I needed to. The worse I felt internally, the happier I would appear outwardly. *I can do this.*

Resolving Family Turmoil

I was only at work for about a week or so before I took time off to visit my mom. Now that both her parents had passed, she had a home full of memorabilia she had to sort through. I flew down to Virginia to give her the support I couldn't give her at the funeral. Historically, when we greeted each other in the terminal, she practically jumped up and down when she saw me coming out of the gate. This time, it was evident she was devastated and exhausted, her eyes sunken in, completely spent. I could also see her disappointment in me. We didn't even say hello. We just hugged and started walking together in silence. My sister Maria was waiting for us at my mom's house. She was also visibly depleted. I barely had a chance to hug her when my mom said, "Theresa, it was so hard. It was so hard and I needed you there. I needed you." She began to cry. She cried and she cried like I'd never seen before, and there was nothing I could do. I had let her down and my punishment was to just stand there helplessly while my mother fell apart in front of me. I choked back my own tears, knowing that my pain would only make hers worse. Eventually, I hugged her and didn't let go until she subsided; there was nothing I could say.

We entered my grandparent's former home with the intent to clear it out. It was a slow process to start. It seemed my mom was attaching sentiment to every inanimate object. "Look, grandma's phonebook." At this rate, we would end up keeping everything. I suggested to my mom that we take a picture of all the artifacts that reminded us of Grandma and Papa and then make a digital scrapbook including all of them. That way we can get rid of all the items but still have the memories associated with them. This sat well with my mom as she loves photography and she is an avid scrapbooker. As the three of us worked through the entire house, deciding what to keep, what to give away, and what to throw away, I felt my mom slowly forgiving me.

A few days into the daunting chore, we took a break and went to lunch at a restaurant with lovely outdoor seating that reminded me of the Camino. It was at that time, sitting in the summer heat, that I confided in my mom and my sister that I was struggling tremendously. I broke down in tears, telling them I didn't understand what was happening to me but that nothing felt right anymore. I went into detail about my Camino experiences and tried to figure out what was leaving me so distracted but kept coming up with nothing. They were very supportive, although without any answers, and by the time I left Virginia my mom told me she understood why I couldn't make it to the funeral, and that I shouldn't beat myself up over it anymore; she forgave me. Hearing that was a tremendous relief and allowed me to begin working through my own grief without guilt overwhelming the process.

Seeking Comfort from Trail Family

I returned home feeling as though I did all I could to handle my grandma's death and all the horrible business associated with losing a loved one. I paid my respects and I made peace with my mom. I was hoping to move on quickly.

But I soon realized I was dealing with another source of grief. I missed my Camino friends and all the amazing people I spent so much time with. I was always fascinated by the concept of a "trail family" and I was intrigued by the relationships Brian formed while on the AT. When I left for the Camino, I hoped to make similar connections. But like with most aspects of trail life, because the Camino was so much shorter in time and distance than the AT, I assumed that I would not have similar experiences to Brian.

What I learned is that "tramilies" are a fundamental aspect of trail life. The people you hike with have an enormous impact on your trail experience, so it's important you spend your time with people you enjoy being around, who make you happy, and who inspire you. This happens very organically. On the Camino, I never gave this aspect much thought beyond knowing that I enjoyed the company of others. Throughout my days, I would run into people from time to time. They would pass me, I would pass them, we'd run into each other while taking a break at one of the cafes, and we'd have dinner and drinks together at night. The interactions were always heartwarming and exceptionally honest. Apparently, when strangers meet on a sacred trail, they're compelled to share who they truly are, free from fear of judgement. This kind of openness, while completely unusual anywhere else in the world, is the norm on the Camino. It lends itself to deep binding relationships quickly formed between strangers from different walks of life. Soon you begin seeing these people in all of their imperfect humanity and you begin to love and respect them for exactly who they are. They become an instrumental part of your journey as you equally share the intense physical, mental, and spiritual strain of the Camino. You're all experiencing powerful personal changes but together in each other's company.

I acquired numerous amazing Camino friends over my 38-day journey. As I realized my people at home couldn't relate to me anymore, I sought comfort from my Camino friends and family who I quickly learned were dealing with similar symptoms of "trail blues." I stayed in touch with Nikolai, Melisa, and Ginger the most and our relationships continued to grow after the Camino in different ways over time. We all had a re-adjustment phase to contend with and everyone found ways to cope. For example, my friend Tina was desperate to return to the Camino, and did so, as many pilgrims do, a number of times over the next few years. My online Camino network was extensive and I watched reunions play out all over the world as people traveled far and wide to reunite with their families and relive the best days of their lives together.

I took comfort in knowing that I wasn't the only one to return home feeling somewhat lost. Some of my friends processed what they were going through very privately and withdrew from everyone which was sad and disappointing for me but most of us talked about it openly, shared how much we missed each other, how others didn't seem to understand us, and how we longed to be back on the Camino but couldn't really explain why. This made me feel normal, although it did not make me feel better.

Moving On

The months dragged on in a fog, feeling alienated and detached from the world around me. My depression was so overwhelming, I couldn't even be reached by my loving husband who had a sense of what I was going through. I remember lying in bed one morning, unable to get up for the day. Brian was standing over me, trying to encourage me to move, but he wasn't getting through to me. I remember him saying, "I'm right here, Theresa. Where are you?" I was so far removed from reality.

I hated going to bed at night because I knew it would feel like only seconds later when I would wake up and have to survive yet another day. I would be forced to conduct a series of familiar but seemingly pointless motions to get ready for work. "Now I have to brush my teeth. Now put the toothpaste back in the drawer. Now I have to wash my face." As I stared at the shell of a person staring back in the mirror, I counted every step, and with each one I accomplished I told myself I was surviving. I had to take life one minute at a time. I felt physical pain but couldn't describe where or why, and my only relief from that pain was in those first few seconds in the morning when I awoke. It took about that long before I was jarred into consciousness, reality set in, and the dark depression descended over me. Things were quite bleak for a while.

Over time, I began to slowly find myself again, but the woman I found was different now. My core was still there, but some of the "fuzzy" aspects of myself became more clearly defined, more complete. Brian and I stayed in close touch with the Camino and AT communities and each September our best friend Matt would join us to set up a camp along the AT in Maine, offering much needed trail magic to the dozens of thru-hikers passing by over the course of three days. I enjoyed spending time with hikers; they were my people.

Having the opportunity to talk to many long-distance hikers helped me define my own experiences a bit more. I realized one thing that unequivocally occurs with each of us: when you have an experience like this, you do not come back the same person. I cannot emphasize that enough. *You do not come back the same person.*

It also occurred to me that this phenomenon probably does not only apply to long-distance hikers. World travelers, people returning from war, women having recently given birth, young adults returning home from college; there are so many life altering experiences we endure, and are then thrust back into our former lives and expected to thrive. That's not to say that these events are comparable but the commonality they share is that the individual does not come back the same.

Perhaps it occurs in different ways for each person, but for me, returning from the Camino I had an overall different outlook on the world and more importantly, my role in it. I began to realize that what made this change most difficult and why I felt so flustered upon my return, is that everyone around me expected me to be the same I was before. So not only was I actively living against those expectations, but I felt alienated by the fact that everyone who I had come to know and love over the years no longer knew me. Once I was able to understand this, I was able to start working towards feeling better about it and ultimately, the benefits far outweighed the difficult times. The Camino taught me what kind of person I want to be, what kind of life I want to live, and what kind of world I want to live in.

The "Life Changes" Phenomenon

Between the months of July and October, Brian and I loved to visit the small town of Rangeley, Maine. During this time of year, the town is full of AT thru-hikers who stop for provisions and rest before tackling some of the toughest terrain of the AT and before they summit Mount Katahdin. During those months, Brian and I love to buy ourselves large iced coffees and drive between downtown Rangeley and the trailhead, which sits about eight miles south of town, and pick up AT hitchhikers. We especially enjoy doing this on rainy days because anyone who saves a hiker from spending any time in the rain at all is a true "trail angel" and because ever since Brian hiked for two months straight in the rain, he becomes chronically sad whenever the weather turns. He has to remind himself that he doesn't have to walk in it anymore and sometimes the only thing that gets him out of bed is the promise of a gallon of caffeine and time with thru-hikers!

When we pick up hikers, we generally have about ten minutes to get to know them before we drop them off at one of the hiker hostels, the laundry mat, the grocery store, or wherever they need to go. In this time, we learn where they're from, their trail name, what condition their bodies are in, and any major events that have occurred during their trek. Through this experience, Brian and I both feel we are reconnecting fondly with our time spent hiking. I also find it healing because I was and continue to be frequently reminded that many long-distance hikers experience similar struggles when they return home. In fact, to sum up how many post hikers feel about their new outlook on life, I'll quote one thru-hikers in particular. We explained to the gentlemen that we have both hiked multiple long-distance trails over the last few years. He himself was on his third thru-hike and he asked, with complete sobriety, "So, how has hiking ruined your life?" Those poignant words rang in my ears for weeks. Why is it that so many people struggle so immensely after a long-distance hike? Furthermore, how do we learn from this struggle to better our lives?

I believe the answer is that while we are off hiking or traveling for pleasure, we experience the world as we are meant to, but when we return to "real life" we realize our world is moving needlessly fast. It's painfully alienating, and unnecessarily harsh. I also believe it is for this reason that many people return to their "real life" and make major changes. Let me be very clear about this point. I am not suggesting that everyone who hikes returns to abandon their former life. However, it has been my experience that many people who return to lives that no longer fulfill them tend to make changes. They get new jobs, new homes, new hobbies, new significant others. They purge their former lives of anything that no longer serves their new outlook on life in an effort to find balance they might never have noticed they were lacking. While hiking the Camino, once I became comfortable with my surroundings, my body was working well for me, and my mind was in a good place, I found myself asking profound questions: "What is my purpose in life? Am I living my life right? Am I being my best self?" When I returned home, those questions persisted. I was forced to reassess every aspect of my life that impacts who I am and the person I want to be.

I noticed several people in Brian's circle of friends made major life changes following their hike, but I did not fully appreciate the depths of those life-changing decisions or how fortunate I was that Brian did not make any of his own major changes. Yes, he slightly altered his employment situation, but he did not move to another country, and most importantly, he did not leave me. It was only after my Camino that I realized that was a very real possibility. I learned through my own experience that when you have a life-changing adventure, your eyes are opened to the endless opportunities in this world. Suddenly you realize you are bound by nothing; you are bound by no one. This new realization forces you to rethink your choices you have made for yourself.

How do you spend the majority of your time? Is it fulfilling? Does it make an impact?

Who are you spending your time with? Do they nourish you? Do you love them? Do they fulfill your needs? Are they making your life better?

Where do you spend most of your time? Is it a healthy environment? Do you feel safe and comfortable?

All these questions run through your head, and some may pass quickly as the answers are clear, but others may rock you to your core. I was forced to work through every one of these questions in excruciating detail and it was an exercise in strength and courage. I was forced to face myself on the Camino, and it seemed that I would be once again upon my return. Brian went through a similar exercise when he returned, but he did so privately, so I wasn't fully aware it was going on. Even after I returned from my own journey, it took a solid two years to even recognize I was going through this exercise.

Redefining Relationships and Cultivating Meaningful Connections

If there is one thing I think all long-distance hikers, long term travelers, and anyone else who chooses to adventure can agree on, it's that when we return many of our relationships are affected. I mentioned the story of when I went to dinner with my friends and felt a sudden disconnect. I would learn over the course of the next year that disconnected feeling expanded throughout my entire social network, from my closest friends, to family members, to even my husband. It seems that once something has changed so dramatically internally it becomes very difficult to relate to those around you, those who knew you before. For months, I found I couldn't connect with people, couldn't relate, couldn't get comfortable. Prior to embarking on the Camino, I had many friends, hosted lots of parties, and was rarely alone. But when I returned, the same people I spent all my time with before the Camino, and with whom I was perfectly happy before, no longer made me happy. I no longer felt fulfilled.

At first, I was angry with them. How could I have such amazing personal connections with people on the Camino and come home to people I couldn't connect with at all? I was also no longer interested in the things they were interested in. I found myself profoundly bored with small talk. I remember sitting with my girlfriends at a restaurant one night. They were cooing over my friend's necklace. She was so happy they noticed and described for several minutes about how versatile the necklace was and all the outfits it was compatible with. I stared blankly at everyone who appeared to be so genuinely happy for her and fought back the urge to scream "NOBODY CARES ABOUT YOUR STUPID NECKLACE!!!!"

Realizing temper tantrums would be frowned upon, I withdrew from everyone, angry that they could not relate to me, that they couldn't fulfill my needs (even though I didn't know what those needs were anymore). They seemed less interested in connecting than I was. Why were my relationships suddenly so hopelessly empty?

This is one area where I found a therapist to be very helpful. Sure, you can talk to friends or family, but they tend to introduce unconscious bias that ultimately results in advice that may be more beneficial to them than it is to you. Therefore, when it comes to relationships, I find having an outside perspective from someone who has nothing to gain to offer support. Having a third party help me navigate these relationships enabled me to identify why I was struggling so immensely and how to manage that in a healthy way. It took me probably over a year to slowly learn that the problem was not that my friends had changed, but that I had. Not only was I a different person now, but no one understood that about me. I had lived, loved, and learned in ways that many people never have the opportunity to. More importantly, my needs had changed. Rather than the light-hearted shallow talk I needed prior to the Camino, I now craved deep, meaningful connections. I also realized it wasn't fair of me to expect my social network to change just because I had. Because the people you meet on the Camino create the experience you have while hiking, it is important to be particular about who you surround yourself with. This is not only true while hiking but in all facets of your life.

I began to painstakingly consider each relationship and determine which ones were worth maintaining and which were no longer serving a need. I found that regardless of how long I'd known someone, whether they were friends, neighbors, or relatives, some people were worthy of my time, love, and devotion while others simply were not. With some relationships, I found the need to devote more care and interest while in others, I found them to be draining and unnecessary. And where I remained completely unfulfilled, I began cultivating new relationships with other people.

I had this new need to be challenged, I needed to be around people who would force me to think outside of my usual self, people who would introduce me to new things, people who would force me to grow and people who would be genuinely interested in joining me in that process. I sought those people out and made them a part of my life. I also learned the value in briefly chatting with complete strangers. There is so much you can learn from even the smallest interactions with people and suddenly I was taking notice of strangers around me whom I wouldn't have given a second glance previously. Eventually, I learned to accept and maintain my previous relationships for what they were, realizing that while not all relationships give you everything you need, there is indeed value in everyone you know, and there is always something you can offer them in return.

While this exercise in personal relationships was difficult and sometimes lonely, the lessons I learned about building healthy and balanced connections with others is yet another lifelong gift I never would have known had the Camino not inspired me to want more out of life.

Strengthening My Marriage

I cannot talk about relationships without talking about the profound impact my journey had on my relationship with my husband. My marriage was not exempt from the mental gymnastics I had to do in determining which relationships were meeting my needs. Brian and I have both learned some extremely important lessons over the last few years.

I think from the outside looking in, many people have questioned the nature of our relationship even prior to our hikes. When I began telling people Brian was going to hike the Appalachian Trail, I was surprised that the majority of responses were something like, "How can you let him leave you for so long?" *Let him?* This baffled me. I'm not his keeper. I can't make him do anything. And he wasn't *leaving* me. He was living his life. As his spouse, I believe I am the one person in the world who should be encouraging him to be a better person and to find his passion in life. In a world filled with responsibilities, chores, careers, and people constantly telling us what we should and should not be doing, I felt like I should be that one person on his side, advocating and encouraging him, supporting his dreams. And I had no doubts he would do the same for me. Even when I was planning my Camino, I often heard people say things like, "yes, but he left for six months. It's not really fair that you only get to leave for two." It seemed that people were wholly focused on "fairness" and keeping score. But that was never really how either or us viewed marriage and I am dubious of others who do. Instead, we both took a leap of faith by encouraging the other person to experience the world individually and patiently awaiting the other's return. I am so grateful that Brian and I have both had the opportunity to have these experiences because although we did them separately, they have ultimately made us closer and stronger.

It didn't start like that though. When Brian returned from the AT, I couldn't possibly understand what he had been through and I didn't understand just how much he had changed. I don't even want to think of how our relationship might have stagnated had we not found a way to relate to one another again. But, although we had these two wildly different experiences, although we have walked different paths (both literally and figuratively), when we returned, we still found one another. Initially, there was a period of time when we felt distant from one another as we processed our journeys but, in both cases, we reconnected.

After Brian's trip, we reconnected through the discovery that our lives were just better together, and after my trip, we reconnected on an even more profound level because we now had common life-changing experiences to draw from. These experiences were loving gifts and tangible evidence of our selfless love. Today, we have a deeper love and admiration, not only because we learned to grow separately but in parallel with one another, but because we encourage and support one another rather than allowing jealousy, resentment, and other negative emotions fuel our marriage.

Following his trip, Brian had a ravenous thirst for outdoor adventures, travel, and communication with those he met on the AT. I didn't have a problem with any of these things, but because I could not relate I felt a bit left out or disconnected from whatever he was going through. Nonetheless, I learned it was important to pay attention to this new Brian. What seemed like small details to me equated to massive changes for Brian. For example, while hiking the AT, he would frequently sit on large rocks alongside lakes and stare across the water for long periods of time. I didn't understand how pivotal these moments were for him until he began talking about wanting to quit his job and move to a quaint trail town such as Rangeley, Maine which features a beautiful pristine lake, and of course lots of large rocks to sit on. Granted, we did not have a big rock overlooking water at our home but I still liked the life we worked so hard to build despite that minor detail. So why would either of us want to change that? We struggled with this sudden difference in what we wanted out of life. He took me to the small town once, hoping I would fall in love with it as he did. We hiked up Saddleback and Brian got teary eyed, reminiscing as we stood at the summit. Admittedly, when I saw Brian all emotional atop that mountain my instinct was to roll my eyes and push onward. But despite not understanding him, that response felt cruel so instead, I waited quietly as he recounted memories to me.

It didn't help the poor guy's case that he brought me to his favorite trail town on a bleak, overcast November day when the town was essentially closed and the lake he spoke so fondly of was not visible through the fog. "Brian, this place sucks." I dismissed any talk of moving initially, not realizing how important it was for him to stay connected to his trail memories. When I returned from the Camino, I could relate to that draw towards the outdoors and that need to preserve memories in our hearts, so we compromised and decided to buy a tiny one-room cabin that we could retreat to on weekends. Now Brian and I return to Rangeley on a regular basis, which means the world to him. Had I not had a similar experience, I don't think I would have respected his needs the way I do now. It is possible our differing needs could have driven us apart had we not worked so hard to find common ground. I have since also completely fallen in love with the magic of that remote trail town.

Brian was also very patient with me. Just as being outdoors

became important to him, after my Camino I had a desperate need to travel independently. Brian waited patiently at home as I traveled to other states and countries, sometimes alone and sometimes with friends, trying to keep the independence I found on the Camino alive in my spirit. I know through that process some outsiders were judging me for daring to travel without my husband, but the only person's opinion that mattered to me was Brian's, and we were always in sync. With every bit of patience he offered me, the deeper in love I fell with him.

Through this process of reestablishing ourselves together and accepting our newfound selves, we learned some powerful life lessons regarding our marriage. Brian and I learned early on that stable marriages exist between couples who recognize they are two individuals on their own journey. We find love in our similarities and our determination to help the other live our life to the fullest. Love occurs when we realize we can be individuals together. I think a lot of people believe that their spouse should be everything for them and they should always do everything together. We've learned that's simply not true, and in fact this unrealistic expectation can be detrimental to the relationship. We are individuals first. We have different needs, dreams, and aspirations. And while we should not expect the other to provide us with all the happiness in the world, our partners should do everything in their power to enrich our life together. We are both eternally grateful that two individuals having had their own adventures, changing and growing on a daily basis, can still find that which connects us so strongly. We are constantly evolving with every experience so it is continuous work. A stable marriage is not an end state though. It's a continuous evolution, so as we continue to grow and change over time, we must frequently remind ourselves of these lessons if we want to maintain our healthy and happy life together.

About two years after my Camino, Brian and I felt like we had finally reconnected on a whole new level, and in the summer of 2017, we renewed our wedding vows in our backyard with about forty friends as witnesses. Matt officiated the ceremony, and of course the main topic was centered around our newfound adventurous life together. That and barbecue because who doesn't like barbecue?

I'm not suggesting that the only way couples can truly understand each other is for each to embark on a momentous adventure, but what I am suggesting is that when one person returns from such a trip you can expect there to be some adjustments to your lives together and your relationship with one another. I have seen in other couples the struggle they go through as one returns somewhat different than they were before. They have to find each other again, find what they have in common, find what they love about each other. Mutual communication, kindness, and compromise are critical.

A Deeper Connection with God

I felt a great deal of pressure to write something powerful and inspiring with regard to my spiritual connection with God, because the Camino is a pilgrimage and it was indeed a spiritual experience for me. I felt the need to share some deep revelations with my fellow pilgrims to highlight the significance of the Camino in one's life. But if I'm being authentic, the truth is I didn't have any spiritual revelations on the Camino. Yes, I had major realizations about myself, but as for my relationship with God, I feel there were only subtle, albeit important, tweaks to it.

While I consider myself a Christian, I suppose many would argue I'm a poor example of one. I'm not one to participate much in organized religion and I only occasionally attend Mass on Christmas. Overall, I believe a true Christian is measured by her daily actions. How we choose to treat our fellow humans, animals, and environment says more about our beliefs and dedication to God than does the frequency at which we attend services. So, while I've always felt a closeness to God and worked hard to live my life honorably, I could not be mistaken for a traditional Christian. While I was preparing for my Camino, I was actually nervous I might encounter religious "zealots" who would not accept me or bombard me with more spiritual discussion than I was accustomed to handling. I found that not to be the case, as many people were on the Camino for different reasons. Overall, it seemed the younger people I encountered were looking for adventure while the older people were looking for answers. Or perhaps it was the other way around? The reasons varied a lot. That spiritual connection was there when I needed it though. I meditated and prayed in multiple churches and cathedrals daily and pilgrims often talked openly about their faith while walking if you were willing to listen.

While on the Camino I felt very close with God. When you spend hours every day hiking, you have a great deal of time to think and reconnect not only with God but with yourself. I found myself praying for hours. I frequently asked for strength, courage, for purpose, whatever I needed physically, mentally, or spiritually to get me through another day on the Camino. I reached deep within myself and out into the universe for answers on a regular basis. In doing so, I was able to find God and remember that there is something much larger than myself. While I might not understand how, I play an important role in this world. Life is not meaningless and what we do matters! We may not see the effects immediately; sometimes maybe not at all, but it matters. So, forward I walked, praying regularly, and I frequently felt I received the response I needed. This time between us had strengthened my belief in and relationship with God.

That meaningful time altered my day-to-day interaction with God after the Camino as well. Prior to the Camino I prayed regularly but rarely for myself. I'd count my blessings on a daily basis, but the bulk of my praying was for others. On the Camino, I was the first person I'd pray for. I was constantly looking for an array of other traits required to fulfil a long-distance hike. Yet, when I returned home, at first, I reverted to only praying for others. I felt that praying for myself made me ungrateful or whiney. And how could I feel anything other than gratitude for the life I've been given, especially when there were other people and animals who were more deserving of attention? While writing this book, I frequently felt alone, like no one could tell me what the right answer was. Should I be completely honest? Should I only share it with a few friends? Should I burn it and never look back? One of my beloved Camino partners, Ginger, became something of a spiritual mentor for me as our relationship continued to grow over the years. She had a powerful relationship with God and while she admits to being far from perfect, she embodies what I believe to be a true Christian. She attempts to see the best in people, she does not judge, and she's quick to forgive. One weekend during a spontaneous girl's getaway in Maine, she encouraged me to pray for myself and about my book, which up until then I hadn't even considered. So, I began engaging with God again the way I did on the Camino, free from feeling like perhaps I wasn't deserving of God's love and attention. Now I realize I can talk to God whenever I want, and about whatever I want. The only one judging me was myself.

I believe one of the most powerful aspects of the Camino is how simple and sweet life becomes for its pilgrims. Because you don't have the weight of your normal daily responsibilities which are burdensome, difficult, and distracting, your purpose and meaning becomes clearer. Without the fears and insecurities we normally carry, a pilgrim is able to surrender herself to a greater power, whatever she believes that power may be. For some, it may be a man with a white beard; for others, it may be invisible energy that connects all of us fundamentally. On the Camino, pilgrims connect to whatever that higher power is in a profound way.

While I do feel more spiritual now, there was a period of time when I actually felt further from God. I mentioned that immediately following my return from the Camino, I reached out to God but I didn't feel as though I was getting a response. I'm not sure what happened, but those first few months I was totally and utterly alone. Even that strong bond with God seemed to have disintegrated and I had no one to turn to. Ginger told me once that sometimes the Holy

Spirit is quiet and we don't know why, but we have to be ok with that. While I didn't understand it at the time, I think now that I needed to be alone with my thoughts when I returned. I had been through so much and I was growing and changing through each experience. I think I needed those months to adjust to those changes and figure out who I had become and how I'd changed. Sometimes solitude is necessary, whether we prefer it or not. Eventually, the connection to my spirituality began to return in a slightly different way, as did all my other relationships.

It was actually on the Camino that I first understood why for some people, nature is their church. The summit of Mount Katahdin, which is the northernmost part of the Appalachian Trail and considered the proverbial finish line for most thru-hikers, is also a sanctuary for so many people. It is sacred ground for the Abenaki and other indigenous people and is also considered sacred to many in the outdoors community as well. People hike to the summit just to pay tribute. Likewise, in Rangeley, Maine there is a group of mountain bikers who meet for "dirt church" every Sunday morning when they ride into the deep woods of Maine together. As an Italian American, I was brought up in the Catholic Church and there was a time when I would have considered this a mockery to the Church and to God. But I have since come to realize that many people feel closest to God when they are one with nature. I also realized that people connect with God in many different ways and how they choose to do so, as long as they're not hurting anyone, is not really my concern. Also, how fitting is it that when people are surrounded by God's most amazing creations, that they feel closest? I now personally find a deeper connection to God when I'm within nature, more so than I ever did within a building.

Connecting with the Outdoors

While Brian and I valued the importance of spending time outdoors, these values were heightened due to our hikes. Brian's return from the AT came with a deep drive to become one with nature whenever possible. I was quickly warming to this perspective because over the last several years I had been attending an annual state-run program called Becoming an Outdoors Woman (BOW). This weekend event was filled with classes focused on exposing women to the outdoors in a safe and controlled manner. I learned all about hunting, trapping, tracking, fire building, camping, hiking, snow shoeing, campfire cooking, kayaking, wilderness first aid, fly fishing, and a whole range of activities that I thoroughly enjoyed. In fact, shortly after Brian returned from the AT and I was contemplating the Camino, I took a slightly more hardcore outdoor survival class hosted by a different organization. In this course, I had to find water, build a fire from tools I made, and sleep out in the cold woods alone. That evening, as I curled into myself, feeling the hypothermia slowly spread through my body, I downed several chocolate bars knowing my body required loads of calories to maintain a healthy temperature. I felt miserable and it was the longest sleepless night. But the moment I saw a hint of daylight in the distance, I felt like a champion. It occurred to me in that moment that if I could survive a night like that, I could definitely hike the Camino alone. I remember feeling energized and confident.

So, Brian and I were by no means strangers to the outdoors, but it wasn't until I spent 18 hours a day out in the elements that I realized just how healthy, natural, and vital it is for humans to spend time outside, connecting with the world around us. I walked through rain, sun, and mud. I climbed over mountains, walked past streams, and passed through forests and meadows, all the while taking in nature's sights and smells. I mentioned at one point in my journal the moment I was completely awestruck by the beauty around me. "Just look at this! I love this" I blurted. My soul was bursting with joy and contentment simply because I was outside, soaking in the sun and fresh air.

I have since made sincere efforts to spend adequate amounts of time outside. Whether it's taking a walk or merely sitting out on the deck, I schedule time to enjoy nature. Whenever I'm having a rough day, just a few minutes outside can calm my soul as it reminds me that the world is much bigger than whatever small challenge I'm dealing with at the moment.

Honoring Authenticity

While I have learned so many things over the last few years I believe first and foremost the Camino has taught me to accept myself for who I am, and all my imperfections. This meant not only being honest with myself, but being open with those around me about who I truly am. But this shift in thinking did not occur overnight. It was, instead, a slow winding journey that continued after I returned home. I watched and listened in amazement as strangers on the Camino shared the deepest parts of themselves so openly, so freely, without fear of judgement. I wanted to participate but often found myself merely a spectator. I wasn't able to really talk about what was important to me. My concern was always either that no one would be interested in what I had to say, or that if they were interested it was only so they could use it against me. After a great deal of reflection, I realized my guardedness was a key factor in keeping me from connecting with others the way I craved following my trip.

I spent days thinking about this part of myself while on the Camino. Where had I learned to distrust over the years? Why was I so unable to open up to people? One event came to mind almost immediately. It was one of those defining moments in your life that helps shape how you see the world, but you're completely unaware of it at the time.

I was 17 years old and living in my college dorm my first semester in school, on my own and away from home for the first time. Back home, my parents were going through a brutal divorce that ripped through our family like a tidal wave. Everyone was in pain and fighting. I felt truly alone and fearful for my future. I wasn't an adult yet, not ready to be kicked out of the nest, but also old enough that people expected me to behave like one.

There were several times when matters at home seeped their way into my college experience even though I was four hours from all the fighting. There was one particularly poignant evening that came to mind when I reflected deeper on my distrust in sharing with others. I don't even remember the wretched thing that was happening at that particular time, but details aside, what I do remember was feeling overwhelmed and unable to control my life. I sat on the floor of my friend's dorm room and cried openly and painfully. At the time, the boys and girls around me appeared to be supportive and understanding. They told me everything was going to be ok and comforted me with hugs and hot tea. But when I exited my friend's room to return to my own, I saw about a half a dozen people sitting on the floor in the hallway looking up at me. Apparently, my cries could be heard down the hall and they had all come to see the train wreck. I learned later that everyone, including my "friends" had a good laugh at my expense, and from then on, they had very little respect for me or interest in me. Between my absent and tumultuous family at home and my faux friends at school, it was a lonely and dreadful start to my college experience, and when that terrible semester was finally over, I packed my entire dorm room into my tiny car by myself, never said goodbye to a single person, and never returned to that school.

My college experience did improve over the years after transferring schools and maturing a bit, but that moment was pivotal for me. At 17, I had learned a harsh lesson I would carry with me for years. I told myself then that people are not genuinely concerned for others. People are self-centered, self-absorbed, and if they do take interest, it's only for their own morbid curiosity or so they can judge and hurt you. I have frequently recalled that lesson in my life and when I was asked to talk about myself on the Camino, I recalled that memory with pain. I'd quickly push the lesson aside, choosing not to explore those negative thoughts further, but also choosing not to share myself with those around me.

Fast forward to several years after my Camino. I found myself sitting in my therapist's office, explaining with excitement how I intended to document its life-changing effects in my second book. My therapist, whom I started seeing on a weekly basis shortly after returning from the Camino, seemed almost entertained by the idea. She reminded me of a time, just after my Camino, when I was struggling so much with my relationships. She reminded me of one particular visit when she suggested I tell my friends I was having a hard time readjusting to life and reconnecting with them. She encouraged me to stop pretending everything was fine and that perhaps they would understand if I explained what I was going through. I couldn't help but laugh thinking back on that time because I thought her advice was absurd. I had spent so many years hiding weakness and fearing I would be exploited that I refused to imagine life any other way.

Over the course of a few years, I had learned to be more open with my friends and when I look back on the person I was before, I realize just how far I've come and that I have my entire Camino experience to thank for it; not just the trail itself, but the life events that occurred as a result. I hadn't even realized I carried this unhealthy perspective for so many years or that it was keeping me from truly connecting with others. While I documented and published my first book, it honestly never occurred to me that anyone would read it. So, I hadn't taken into consideration just how much people would learn about me by reading it. I didn't realize how much of myself I was sharing. But, as I saw the positive impact of being authentic, that openness and authenticity became a regular part of my life over time.

Following the publishing of my book and after giving dozens of talks, my life became fairly public in small circles. Complete strangers, and even people within my life with whom I never had much of a connection suddenly felt like they knew me, and they wanted to know more. It wasn't that they were interested in me personally, but I think they felt they had something to gain from hearing about someone else's lessons, mistakes, and accomplishments. I've also realized people are hungry for authenticity and they are eager to make connections with others. By removing those proverbial defensive walls around my own life, I've been able to connect with others in ways that were never possible before. Connecting with others is a fundamental part of being human that I believe most of us need and want but often struggle with.

The encouragement to be open continued as I received letters and emails from people from around the world telling me how they too found what amazes them and what inspires their life. It never ceases to amaze me how simply being ourselves can positively impact others. I realized that this is how I can give back to the world, this amazing gift I was given. If offering someone a few words of truth and encouragement is just what they need to do something amazing for themselves, how can I not accept that role?

Being my authentic self also meant honoring the darker parts of my being. This took a bit longer, but eventually I discovered the liberation of acknowledging and embracing my deepest imperfections. "Trail blues" or "trail depression" is so commonly experienced within the community, and yet few people talk about it in depth. I felt I owed it to my readers to be honest about my own experiences in the hopes that others would find comfort knowing they are not alone. But what I didn't expect was that by simply sharing that experience with others back home, I would continue to make unexpected connections. I'm overwhelmed with the openness and honesty I am offered by people now. In return for sharing my story, people often feel empowered to share their own secrets and dreams. It is shocking and disheartening to learn how many people hide themselves so deeply, even from their most loved ones.

Of all the things I've learned people hide from their loved ones, the most prevalent is strained mental health. So many people suffer in silence, and I can relate. I have suffered from depression and anxiety for my entire life, and the one thing I know is true is that when you are not well, about 90% of your energy goes towards hiding it from those around you. You so desperately want to be normal, and you know that those who have never experienced the debilitating effects of depression couldn't possibly understand. At best, they compare the disease to being incredibly sad, which as those of us who suffer know, it's not even comparable. Over the four decades of my life, I've had only a few bouts of depressive episodes, with anxiety rearing its ugly head whenever it felt the inclination. I would go for years feeling fairly normal but always with depression looming over my days, threatening to take over at the slightest unsettling moment. As many of you are aware, this ailment can be triggered by almost anything, so it should have been no surprise to me that an event such as the Camino would be enough to set off a full-blown depression in my life.

To be clear, I am in no way suggesting that those who hike the Camino will come home to a depressive episode. I can only speak to my own experience and if I'm sharing truthfully, I can't leave out the ugly parts. So, while this was my experience, anyone else's return could look drastically different.

While I was learning important lessons about authenticity, there was another pivotal event in my life. One weekend during the winter after I returned from the Camino, a friend of mine took his own life.

When I first heard he had passed away but had not yet heard the details, I was shocked and sad, but when a closer friend informed me that he had in fact died by suicide, I was devastated. I knew what suicide meant. That meant he did not pass quickly, it was not painless, and it was not natural. It meant he suffered for years and finally decided he wasn't willing to put himself through the pain anymore. I was angry at myself, because while we frequently shared our personal hobbies with each other and found commonality in our desire to adventure, I never knew that we had depression in common.

After taking a couple of days off work to process my friend's death, I came to the realization that by hiding my own illness I was not helping this cause. I posted on my social media page that night that I work through depression and anxiety regularly, and that if anyone ever needed someone to talk to, I was there for them. It sounded cliché but it was honest and to my surprise, I received over a dozen private messages from people who admitted to me that they too were in a great deal of pain, and most of them had never told a single person. One woman who had a common but particularly sad story said that she hid her disease from her own husband because he saw depression as merely a symptom of laziness. Meanwhile, a man who I wasn't very close with until that very night informed me that, while he was considered a successful businessman, he frequently has panic attacks in the bathroom at work. My heart ached for these people. They were so alone and I knew what it felt like to have to hide yourself from the world. I promised I would never hide again, or allow anyone to make me feel ashamed of how God made me. It was a continued lesson in honesty, acceptance, and authenticity and I am eternally grateful for it.

This new honesty and acceptance were additionally beneficial for me in that there was something so incredibly liberating about being able to say "This is me, unapologetically. Love me or leave me. God made me what I am, and I'm grateful for it." Furthermore, the fact of the matter is, when we live our true lives, not the one everyone tells us we should live, but our true authentic lives as God intended, we are better able to contribute to the world in a positive way.

A Sense of Adventure

If you told me even months before I boarded that plane for Madrid that I would be spending time walking through a small part of France and most of Northern Spain, I would not have believed you, and I certainly could not have imagined doing it alone. But now that I've had that divine pleasure, I have since developed a voracious appetite for adventure and travel. The world suddenly seems so much larger and smaller all at the same time. Norway, Nepal, the Netherlands, Iceland, Thailand, Australia. I have to see all these places. My home, which was always filled with peace and love, no longer yielded satisfaction by itself. I've always been fascinated with other cultures, but now that I had traveled alone to a country I had never been with a language I didn't really speak, many myths about travel were debunked for me.

I have learned that traveling establishes a level of independence and self-reliance that I don't think you can get any other way. Knowing that you can take care of yourself and get around safely somewhere you've never been before is quite liberating, and I sought that feeling numerous times after my Camino. You learn a lot about yourself in a very positive way when you have to fend for yourself out in the world.

I learned that you don't need to be proficient in a language to get by in other countries. Sure, you're going to have some really uncomfortable moments when you won't understand what is happening or how to get somewhere, but one thing you learn when you travel to foreign places is how to be comfortable with being uncomfortable. You'll learn that it's ok to not be the master of your domain.

I realized that there are millions of people in this world who find traveling outside of their comfort zone to be completely freeing and they incorporate it into their life whenever possible. I've found that Americans especially are accustomed to being surrounded by their own kind. We're such a large country, which makes it more time consuming and expensive to explore other cultures. Most of us are also slaves to our jobs having little time or money for travel. So, in general, Americans just don't do much of it. Whereas in Europe, you can drive a few hours in nearly any direction and often find yourself immersed in a completely different culture. It's just easier. But I love how once you've entered the travel circuit, you never stop meeting new people, you never stop learning about new places and adventures, and your entire life broadens exponentially.

Not to mention, the more you travel, the more connections you make, and the easier it becomes to go somewhere new because you will probably know someone there. I'm laughing as I write this, because I recall a funny example of connections that occurred a couple of years ago when I had a business trip to Australia. We were staying in a small town hours outside of Sydney when I realized I had a friend there! My colleague jokingly said, "You flew to the other side of the world and bumped into a friend at the gym?" YES! That's the best part of traveling!

A similar experience happened to me while in Iceland. I was walking down the streets of Reykjavik when I heard someone sing out my name. I looked down the road and driving by I spotted two wonderful faces. When I was seven I became pen pals with the daughter of my dad's colleague. We stayed loosely in touch over the years, but never planned to run into each other on the streets of Iceland!

Another benefit of traveling far and wide is it exposes you to different ways of living, and different ways of thinking. You are constantly reminded that your way of life is just one possible outcome, and there are many others to choose from. I believe this makes you more grateful for the positive aspects of your life but also helps you to see where others may be doing things better, not only at the individual level, but at a societal level as well. I think it would be foolish not to look at what other countries are doing to see if we can find better ways to improve our quality of life.

So, those are just a few benefits I've discovered from traveling though I could talk nearly forever on this subject. Shortly after the Camino, I began making plans to travel whenever possible, and I set a goal to see two new countries a year. I quickly learned this was less than realistic when you consider the need for vacation time and money, but I took pleasure in planning trips, talking with friends, and exploring future vacation ideas. I had a continuous need to see more of the world. Sometimes Brian was with me, sometimes I'd go with friends, and sometimes I'd go completely alone. It all depended on what kind of experience I was chasing.

With Brian, every trip is carefully planned to maximize fun and interest. Traveling with him is always the best, but I had found the independence in traveling alone to be so gratifying. Plus, the added benefit to being alone is that you never once have to compromise and your time is completely your own. I've been to Sweden, Portugal, and Australia on my own and I have other trips lined up already. With Brian, I explored the Pacific Northwest, Colorado, Austin, and a few other parts of the US we've been wanting to see. Additionally, we met with one of my Camino friend's Stephen and his wife Rachel in Yosemite National Park and hiked about 100 miles of the Pacific Crest Trail together in 2016. My other hiking partner, Nikolai, met me in Iceland for a week and we toured around the northwest parts of the country together in 2017. And in 2019 Brian and I returned to Santiago de Compostela! It is very common for pilgrims to return to Santiago four, five, or six times! By 2019, when we finally got around to hiking the Portuguese Camino, almost all my Camino friends had already returned. We met Brian's AT buddy from Australia who we affectionately call "Vegemite." The three of us spent 12 days hiking from Porto, Portugal to Santiago. The trip was fantastically fun!

As you can imagine, it was nothing like my first Camino though. The second time around felt entirely different because I was more experienced, more aware of myself, and more familiar with the Camino. Although I had never hiked the Portuguese route before, I had grown so much from my first Camino that I was much more comfortable and when I arrived in Santiago for the second time. I felt like a very different person. I wrote the following in my 2019 Camino Portuguese blog:

Santiago was bustling with people. As we approached the square, I noticed we were entering from the opposite side of the cathedral as I did for the Camino Frances. I wasn't expecting it but seeing that cathedral again was breathtaking for a few reasons. First, when I arrived in Santiago four years ago, the building was under serious restoration and the entire front was obstructed by scaffolding and they put up giant images of the cathedral so you could imagine what it should look like. Today, the building was fully restored and visible. It was magnificent! Every little detail, the statues of St. James, the intricate artwork, the massive windows, it was all there. The other reason seeing that cathedral took me breath away is I realized the last time I saw it, I was a very different person and when I gazed upon it, I had no idea that moment marked Minute One of a long process of self-discovery. All well worth it of course but I was struck powerfully by the fact that my last Camino required FOUR years of processing and in the same year I finally came to terms with the self-growth the first Camino bestowed onto me, I returned for another dose.

For Brian and me, adventure doesn't just come in the form of traveling. Our drive to continuously grow and change has permeated all aspects of our life together. So naturally, we're always on the lookout for better opportunities to move somewhere else, take another job, pick up new hobbies, or make new friends. When I first returned from the Camino, my drive for expanding my horizon felt like restlessness and unhappiness because I suddenly felt so unfilled. However, five years later, exploration and adventure have become a normal part of our lives that we utterly love and thrive on. I will never stop moving forward. I will never stop being curious.

Ironically, as I sit here now, ruminating on how much I love to travel, I find myself cooped up in my home for many months as the COVID-19 pandemic rips across the world. I had first recognized this virus would have a dramatic impact on my life when I was returning home from a trip to Sweden the first week of February 2019 and the flight attendants refused to allow anyone on the plane who had been to China in the past two weeks. It was then that I realized this pandemic was worse than a mere mention in a newspaper.

As the weeks followed, all plans of doing anything were cancelled. From our Monday night indoor rock-climbing routine, to a trip to Guatemala; one by one, I watched each of these plans fade into nothingness. At first, I was saddened by the thought of not being able to travel or even visit friends again for what amounted to all of 2020 and beyond. But as I sit here months into a deadly pandemic which has killed nearly 300,000 people just within the United States, I am simply grateful to be healthy and alive and for my loved ones' safety. I do dream of a day when I can travel again, though and this time we've spent in isolation has allowed Brian and I to prioritize what is important to us and consider what we want for ourselves in the future. We have decided that we'd love to spend more time experiencing our own great nation, and because one unintended consequence of this pandemic is a more remote capable work environment, Brian and I dream of being able to work while we travel around the country, seeing sights, exploring natural wonders, and visiting distant relatives. The dream is far off into the future but it keeps us inspired and gives us the goals we need to preserve through this difficult time in history.

Finding Purpose in Life

Of the 3,000+ pictures I took while on the Camino, there is one of great significance to me. At a glance, there's nothing amazing about it. It was a quick shot I took of Cirauqui, Spain, a small town Melisa and I approached around day seven. The foreground is a bit dark but off in the distance, you could see the small town highlighted in the sun's afternoon rays. That simple photo makes my heart swell whenever I see it, so much that I included it in my presentations, but I didn't really understand why. One day while I was presenting for probably the 20th time, I pulled that image up onto the big screen and the significance of it hit me in a way that I could articulate its meaning to my audience.

One of the greatest things about hiking the Camino is that every day, you have a goal. You wake up in the morning having no idea where you'll be at the end of the day. You review your map, pick an unknown location in the distance and then you strive and work and toil all day to reach that destination. When you arrive, regardless of your physical and mental condition, you feel like a Rockstar, you feel accomplished. You feel as though you have purpose.

Many people (myself included) come home from an adventure like this and feel they have no purpose. We're suddenly bombarded with millions of decisions and choices throughout the day, none of which actually amount to anything important. Pilgrims often return finding they must have purpose in life. It is so important that you continue to ask yourself the tough questions you asked yourself while hiking. What is my purpose? What is the meaning of it all? Why am I here?

I believe I began recovering from my post-Camino fog when I was able to find purpose again. My purpose is to inspire and encourage people to do the things they've always dreamed of but for whatever reason haven't accomplished. Yeah, it's a small thing. I won't cure cancer, I won't solve world hunger. But for most of us, our purpose is to improve the lives of those around us however we can, which can have an enormous impact. For me, encouraging people to be their best self is my small way of giving back and working towards making this world one I want to live in. Most recently I began toying with the idea of becoming a Life Coach. Coaches don't give advice or offer some magical cure. Rather, life coaches offer people the tools they need to unlock what's important to them in life, to set goals, build a plan for reaching their goals, and help hold them accountable for their progress. I've come away from the Camino with so many life lessons and healthy tools that I incorporate into my daily routine. I'd love to more formally help others reach their maximum potential and reap the benefits of those life lessons without necessarily having to walk across a country themselves.

I've learned that I can do this, not only through telling stories of my many adventures but also through listening to people's dreams, encouraging them to identify what's holding them back, and offering any support I can. Those dreams may be personal, work related, it doesn't really matter. They're all important. For example, I met one man who randomly picked up my book one day. It inspired him and his wife to hike the Camino, and while they were out on their trek, they decided to set their lifelong dream of building a lip balm company into motion! This sounds so random and unexpected, but how wonderful! Now, that couple is out there, doing their thing, making amazing lip balm. And I know because they sent me samples!

Everyone was put on this earth to offer something and the fact of the matter is when we are living our best lives we are better able to connect with those around us and contribute to the world. For me, I was named after St. Theresa, "Saint of the little ways." She believed that it's the little things we do to change the world. I embrace that sentiment fully now. For anyone who may be struggling right now, my advice to you is to find your purpose. How can you contribute?

Taking Care of Myself

Our mind and body are our greatest assets. While I was on the Camino, I became very in tune with both. I relied on them for everything, I pushed myself to my absolute limit, I learned to take care of myself, and mourned when I would unintentionally hurt myself. Through that long, difficult, 38-day exercise, I became extremely self-aware both physically and mentally.

Your Body is God's Greatest Gift to You

I learned to love, respect, and appreciate my body on the Camino as I became very familiar with it. It is the greatest gift God has given me and it is what allows me to experience the world the way I am meant to. In a world of body shaming and judgement, this realization is a powerful tool for me. This is something women in particular struggle with every minute of the day. People's bodies are scrutinized on an hourly basis. Every minute of every day, people are looking at us and making value judgments. Sometimes you can ignore it, but it's always there and the pressure is unfair. It's empowering to realize that what others think does not actually matter.

As a 4'7" woman, I'm no stranger to prejudice and body shaming. People often expect very little from me and they almost always assume they are better than me simply because I'm small, until I prove my worth. I've always personally enjoyed being small. It makes me uniquely "me". I've always ignored the rude comments or stupid jokes, knowing those statements are more a reflection of the people saying them than me. But it is frustrating when people assume to know more about me without bothering to get to know me first. I attended a banquet of Camino pilgrims prior to my trip so I could meet others who had taken to the trail and ask for advice. I met a gentleman who was kind and helpful, but when I told him I planned to hike the Camino alone he swatted his hand through the air, shook his head in disbelief and said, "Oh no, you won't be able to do it alone. Find someone to go with you." I don't actually know his reasons for assuming that, but this man knew nothing about me at all, and yet he was confident I would fail. This disbelief continued even once I returned from the Camino. I frequently gave talks at libraries, and I'd stand in front of the audience with the librarian waiting to begin the presentation. Undoubtedly, someone would always approach both of us, and regardless of the librarian's age or physical condition, people always assumed the librarian was the hiker and they were visibly shocked when I corrected them and said that I was in fact the pilgrim. I was always a bit miffed at how surprised people were. People also have a tendency to assume I must not like being small because they themselves perceive it as a negative thing. After decades of these assumptions, I've learned to dismiss them one at a time, but they are persistent and frustrating nonetheless. Realistically, while I've always known that people are grossly wrong to assume smaller means inferior, I constantly had to defend my body and my worth. So, I'm no stranger to body shaming.

When I was on the Camino, I was continuously reminded of how strong and powerful I am. I hiked over the steep Pyrenees Mountains. I slogged through rain and mud. I hobbled dozens of miles on painful blisters, and I scorched in the hundred-degree sun. I did all of that myself. It was such an empowering and personal experience. I frequently found myself thanking God for the body he blessed me with. I never could have seen those sights, met those people, or grown the way I did on the Camino, if I did not have this amazing perfect body to carry me through it. I now despise body shaming of any kind. We are all gifted with a unique body and it's so important that we embrace our strengths and give compassion to our weaknesses. It's important to be grateful for what we've been given regardless of our size, shape, or ability.

Having pushed myself to my limits on the Camino, I have also gained an appetite to challenge myself to find ways to push myself now that I've returned. Prior to the Camino, I was not very physically active. I always dreamed of being physically strong and athletic but I never had the drive or know-how to get there. Now, I feel as though I don't have a choice. Upon returning from what became my first of multiple long-distance hikes, I felt a perpetual need to move, to be active, to revisit my limits. I began working out regularly and taking on new hobbies that required exertion. I took up mountain biking, aerial yoga, rock climbing, and competitive pole fitness all in an effort to take care of myself, strengthen my body, and keep my mind at ease. I saw the circus arts as a new passion through which I could push my limits further than ever before. I set a goal to compete in a pole competition the year I turned 40. I traveled to aerial camps to learn from professionals, made friends from around the world, became very physically fit, and found a creative outlet. I was completely in love with my new hobby.

This new physical lifestyle didn't happen immediately following my Camino though. Like with most of my Camino gifts, things got worse before they could get better. In fact, upon my immediate return, I gained nearly 30 pounds which is quite a bit on my smaller frame. A large part of the excessive weight gain was due to the sudden lack of daily hiking which is something most long-distance hikers have to manage carefully. In addition to the lack of activity, I was also probably eating more than my sedentary life could support. But the weight gain fed my need to be physically active even further and that latent need became so strong that eventually I broke down and bought myself a treadmill to fit under my desk in my home office. Fast forward several years later and I now walk 6-10 miles while working some days. Thanks to the Camino, I now have a very active and healthy lifestyle which I enjoy immensely and I feel amazing.

Another God-Given Gift: Your Mind

Over time, I began to recognize the powerful connection between mind and body and learned that maintaining a healthy mental state proved to be equally important in terms of finding balance. I needed to nurture my mind and body equally. So, in addition to adopting a more physically active lifestyle, I looked for ways to minimize stressors and unnecessary stimulants throughout the day and focused on activities that made me feel more stable.

I began incorporating meditation into my daily schedule. In the beginning, I didn't notice much of a change and I simply closed my eyes and listened to a 5-minute guided meditation app I stumbled across. I tried to do this twice a day but I didn't put much thought into whether or not it was benefiting me in any way. I would close my door at work or lie in bed, close my eyes, and listen to the soothing voice. At first, I used the time as a way to escape from whatever was going on around me. Those few minutes of silence took me back to that time on the Camino when I was free of burdens, stress, chores, tasks, and errands. But after several months of doing this, I began to notice I could tap into that calmness even when I wasn't listening to the recording. The more I practice this meditation, the faster I can find that calm state on tough days. By practicing meditation when it's easy and relaxing, I'm better prepared to call on that skill during more difficult times. It's almost as though

I'm flexing a muscle and my mind remembers how to take a quick moment to bring myself back into focus.

Meditation takes time and practice but that's just one technique I learned to harness over the years. Some others are much easier to get used to and incorporate into your daily routine. Throughout my day, I conduct a series of mental activities, checking in on myself regularly to determine how grounded I am and if I'm finding the balance I need to live fully and comfortably. I literally talk to myself throughout the day, ask how I'm doing and if I'm struggling, I ask myself to identify the source and think of ways to minimize the cause. I found that managing time and stress is critical. When I'm overwhelmed, I prioritize my needs and look for shortcuts. Do the dishes really need to get done today? Probably not. Do I need to take a few minutes to settle my mind and spend quality time with loved ones? Definitely!

I've also discovered that routine is critical to building healthy habits. I always have a healthy achievable goal that I'm interested in and I build routines around working towards that goal. This keeps me focused, engaged, and encourages healthy habits. Of course, I must sprinkle in some spontaneity along the way to keep things interesting without derailing my plans altogether.

I cannot stress enough the importance of being kind to yourself. Like most people I used to be unnecessarily hard on myself. But with practice, I've learned how to treat myself more like how I would treat a friend. That means when I hit a tough part of my life and I'm struggling mentally, I allow myself time and space to not be so rigid. Sometimes life gets in the way of working towards those goals that keep us balanced. Sometimes things become so stressful or busy that it's just too difficult to take care of myself. During those times, I tell myself it's ok to not get everything just right. Maintaining balance is a full-time job, and sometimes I just need a break. Allowing yourself permission for these temporary lapses makes it easier to get back on the wagon when you're able to again.

In addition to all these routines and goals I've built for myself, I've also taken a few cues from my European friends in an effort to maintain mental fortitude. Americans are absolutely obsessed with productivity. We must always be busy, we must always be doing something. What many of us fail to realize is this constant pressure to be productive creates unnecessary stress and is often counterproductive. I now build time into my week to be completely useless and it's quite fabulous. I'll have an espresso and sit in front of the fire pit for a couple of hours or I'll walk into the woods with my dog, find a place to sit, and just be with myself as I did in the wheat fields of Spain. If you're as addicted to productivity as I am, I highly recommend scheduling time to do nothing. This does not mean vegging out in front of the television. Forget about TV; turn off Netflix for a while. There's nothing there for you. Find time and space to just be.

It took time, but eventually, I found myself in a more peaceful state of mind than I ever had prior to the Camino. It wasn't until I gave respect, love, and support to both my mind and body that I truly began to recover from the difficulty of returning from a life-changing adventure and began reaping the benefits of it.

I Can't "YET"

I recently came across a saying that would have sounded cheesy to me before the Camino, but now speaks volumes and I'm reminded of it often: "The only reason it's impossible is because you haven't done it yet." Why does this simple saying mean so much to me now? Well, let's break it down.

Impossible means it can't be done. *Can't*: not possible, impossible. Suggesting something will never ever occur. Sounds like a total downer. But the second part is what psyches me up and sends excitement through my bloodstream. "You haven't done it yet." *Yet!* meaning it's NOT actually impossible. Not only is it completely possible, but it's going to be new and potentially thrilling when you finally accomplish it. The only reason you think something is impossible is that you haven't proven to yourself that you can yet!

Prior to my Camino experience, I frequently felt as though I could not do things. "I can't" was a common theme in my narrative and there were no emotions associated with that sentiment; it was just a matter of fact. It took walking across France and almost the entire length of Spain to gain the confidence to realize that in most cases, that's simply not true. What I've learned from that magical challenge is that we're capable of so much more than we ever give ourselves credit for. I think it's normal for us to spend portions of our time imagining doing incredible things. And when we think of these things, there's often a sense of "Oh, that's just a daydream," and we don't do much to turn that dream into reality.

But that's the difference between people who have amazing

adventures and everyone else. This is the ONLY difference between doers and dreamers. Something inside doers makes them realize they ARE capable. And there's something about doers that others don't understand. Those who do, fail on a regular basis. Not just "Oh, I had a bad day once." They fail a lot. Because with every failure, they know they're getting stronger, they're getting better, they're better prepared for whatever comes next. They're also becoming more resilient. I realized this especially when people refer to me as a natural at something. This always bothers me because assuming someone is a "natural" dismisses all the hard work, dedication, and failure they endured to get to where they are. We all start at the beginning.

I've met hundreds of people who want to take an adventure similar to the Camino or have this great idea for a book they want to write and publish. They come to me seeking advice, and I offer as much encouragement and support I can. But the truth is, I know that while some of these people are doers, the majority are dreamers. And dreams are wonderful! They're where you find inspiration and motivation. But accomplishment requires action. All too often, people are paralyzed with fear, doubt, and laziness. These three human components are destroyers of creativity, discovery, and accomplishment, and I see it frequently in those who dare to dream but fear to execute. I learned through my experience with the Camino and all subsequent adventures that 98% of the time, "can't" is just fear, doubt, or laziness. I didn't think I could walk across a country alone, but I did. I didn't think I could write a book, but I did. I didn't think I could be a public speaker, but I am. I didn't think I was strong, but now I'm a competitive athlete. So, now I have all these examples of how "can't" is just a mental barricade and nothing more. Now I look back on those things and I think, "Of course all of those things are part of my reality. That's SO ME!" Whatever made me doubt that? What made me deny myself the benefits of experience? Now, when I dream about something awesome, the thought is no longer accompanied with a dismissive, "I can't actually do that," but rather with a list of constructive questions like "What kind of training or practice do I need to do that? What do I need to know to be good at that and am I willing to put in the time and work to accomplish that?" I recognize now that all current experts and badasses started exactly where I must. It may take time, dedication, and effort, but most things absolutely are not impossible. This may seem like a subtle difference in how I think now, but ultimately, it's a life altering shift in how I perceive the world, which in turn, alters how I experience it as a whole. The world is literally my playground, and there are thousands of things I could do with my time here. Now it's just a matter of prioritizing and finding time to fit it all in!

Another shift in thinking is how I perceive the process of challenge. You know that saying, "It's not about the destination, it's about the journey?" Yep, that's another saying that makes so much sense to me now. I could have flown directly to Santiago de Compostela and stared up at that cathedral with all the other pilgrims, (and many people do that) but it wouldn't have meant anything. It was all the painstaking effort I spent trying to walk there that made that final moment so magical. After endeavoring for 38 days for a five-minute finale, I have a new respect for persistence and patience. Don't get me wrong. I'm still a product of the instant gratification era, for sure, but when it comes to striving for a goal I'm well aware that to truly be good at something or to truly receive the benefits of an experience, you must respect the process. For example, when I was working towards publishing my first book, every hour that I slaved away on it I was plagued with negative thoughts, "I can't do this, it's too big of a project!" But as I've begun processing my lessons from the Camino and applying them to my current life, my perspective has changed. With this book, I was content with the fact that it could be months or even years before it felt complete and that was ok! The "end" was not my ultimate goal. I was happy with the slow process because I was gaining so much from it. This is my life and I'm not about to hurry through it just to say I've accomplished something. I'm going to enjoy its various stages and learn as much as I can along the way. The Camino has taught me to value experience over accomplishment.

Here's an example of when this new perspective gave me clarity and helped me make the best decision for myself. A year after I hiked the Camino, Brian and I were hiking the John Muir Trail (JMT), a strenuous 200-mile hike in the wild Sierra mountains in California. We were about 100 miles in and Brian and I were not enjoying ourselves for a myriad of reasons. We spent hours contemplating our situation, and in the end, we decided we didn't want to continue the hike to Mount Whitney as planned. We'd spent months planning and paying for this trip, but now it didn't feel right. We told our two hiking partners we would be parting ways the next morning and heading to the nearest town. Our friend seemed genuinely confused. "But...don't you want to see if you can make it to the end?" I was struck at that moment with the contentment and confidence I felt. While on the Camino, I frequently felt the need to prove something to myself, that I could hike the entire trail. Now, through my adventures and challenges, I rarely feel a sense of "can't" so I don't have much need to prove otherwise. I know I can. The question is now, do I want to? I was not hiking the JMT just to reach the summit. I was hiking it to enjoy the experience and the fact was I just wasn't enjoying it anymore. So, it was an easy decision. Had I not had that perspective, I may have forced myself into days of misery just to make an unnecessary point to myself.

Granted, there are still places in my life where this new thinking does not seem to apply. My anxiety and lack of confidence is still alive and well in certain parts of my life, but now I have a framework for working through those areas where I still struggle. I am free to take my destiny into my own hands, free from the burden of having to prove anything to anyone and free from feeling like I can't.

Being Present

While I'm talking about mental states, I'd love to share with you the exceptional mental work one experiences when hiking. I found that during the first couple of weeks of my Camino, my mind was taking me to all kinds of crazy places. I'd focus on the strangest thoughts for days and occasionally I would catch myself. "Why the heck have I been obsessing over superheroes for the last three days? I don't even like comics!" But I hadn't had much experience managing my thoughts up until that time in my life, so I just watched them come and go like strangers passing through a train station. But something happened several weeks in. My mind began to quiet. My thoughts became more streamlined; this is the experience many hikers talk about when they find themselves deep within their mind.

About two thirds of my way across Spain, during one of my unique stops on the Camino, I came across a Camino angel handing out snacks to hungry and tired pilgrims. What made this stop most memorable, besides the seemingly endless flow of watermelon, oranges, and refreshments, was that this special angel built a stand where he shared all his great treats. Painted in Spanish, the stand read, "The key to essence is presence." Of course, like everyone else, I heard of the importance of being "present" but I didn't understand what that meant, how to achieve it, or what the benefits of a present mental state actually were. I couldn't define it and so I wasn't even sure whether I had ever been present in my life.

But, by that point on my pilgrimage, I was beginning to understand what true presence felt like. Hiking day after day, in eight to ten hour stretches, I had a great deal of time to slow my thoughts, take note of the world around me, and reflect. In *Sunrise in Spain,* I wrote about the moment I realized for the first time in my life that I was not mulling over the past or fretting about the future. I was walking in the present and my thoughts were wholly focused on what was happening at the moment. I thought about the rhythm of my heart rate, the sound of my footsteps, the feeling of the ground beneath my feet, the smell of the passing scenery, the breeze brushing across my face, the refreshing taste of the cool fountain water. I felt as though my destination was so far off that I could not see it and I would not arrive any time soon, so it just wasn't much of a concern. When you can't see your destination, you don't have much of a choice but to focus on the here and now.

That experience was remarkable and I still remember taking note of this change in how I was thinking, but even then, I didn't understand the long-term impact that mental process was having on me. Living in the present while hiking may sound like a minor thing, but what I didn't know until much later is that after 38 days of this slow reflection, the Camino literally changed the way my brain functions and how I see the world. I don't know how it happened or even what exactly happened, but when I returned, I felt as though my brain re-wired itself and was now functioning differently. In search of an explanation for what had changed in me, I began reading about neuroplasticity, which is the brain's ability to change its structure and function in response to experience. Today, I process time and space very differently than I did prior to my pilgrimage.

This new mental state wasn't an instant gift, however. In fact, those several weeks after I returned from Europe, I felt the exact opposite about processing time and circumstance. Quite the contrary, I had absolutely no sense of time. My life seemed to be passing at an alarming rate, experiences were flying by, and suddenly my life felt meaningless. I felt absent from my own life, barely having the time to connect with or even observe my life, let alone actively participate. I longed for the ability to slow my mind, slow my daily tasks, so I could take time to appreciate and be grateful for my existence. I had to learn again how to slow down, thank God for my blessings, and be present as I was on the Camino. This was a new lesson I had to incorporate into my life at home because before the Camino, I had never accessed this process. With time and practice though, I was able to not only incorporate my lessons of being present as I was on the Camino, but I also now understand how being present changed how I experience my life as a whole.

Here is what changed. Today, when I think of my life, I see it as a continuum with thousands of phases. Each of these phases may be positive or negative, but either way, they are short lived and will eventually pass. We all know that, sure. But by truly understanding how each event in your life relates to one another, and by taking time to process each in real time, you can decide what type of impact they'll have on you and manage them as needed. For example, when I'm going through a particularly rough time, such as a painful dispute with loved ones, or a difficult challenge at work, or any other event that may wake me in the middle of the night, it used to consume me for weeks. But now, in an effort to better deal with these times in my life, I am able to freeze these moments in my head and take note of the situation, which helps me understand how that moment impacts the grand scheme of things. Is this a memory worth saving? Will this matter in a week? In a month? If not, I'm better able to deal with it and move on by reminding myself that it's merely a phase to be survived and surpassed. As for positive experiences, I'm able to some degree slow that time so I can relish in it and determine how it is benefiting my overall wellbeing. You know that feeling when you've had a great weekend or a vacation and you think "Wow, that flew by"? I don't experience that quite as intensely anymore. Yes, weekends and vacations are never long enough when they're over, but I no longer feel as though I've missed them or that perhaps they went by so quickly I could barely process the time because I was present. I lived and experienced that positive phase the fullest extent possible. So, by learning to be present, I have to some degree been able to manipulate how I experience time and circumstance.

Furthermore, during a normal day, when my situation is neither positive nor negative, I frequently find myself pausing briefly to find gratitude. I think "thank you for this time I have with my husband" or "thank you for this avocado!" These moments aren't forced. They come naturally and whether I'm feeling grateful for the people in my life or the opportunity for a good hearty laugh, the gratitude is genuine and intense. And with each of these instances, I am living very much in the moment.

I've learned that maintaining presence in my life is a lifelong practice that requires continued maintenance. My advice to anyone who hikes the Camino or any other long-distance trail is to allow your mind to wander where it needs to while you are hiking. Don't fight the process. Let your brain do the work, because once it's cleared itself of all the garbage that's rolling around in there, you'll find yourself in a more relaxed and peaceful state. When you return, look for ways to tap into that present state of mind whenever you can.

Navigating Negative Influences

Returning from a blissful, mentally focused state (as you may find yourself on the Camino) to a life riddled with negativity can be quite jarring. I mentioned earlier that we are often paralyzed with fear, doubt, and laziness. What I learned is that not only must we resist these traits in ourselves, but we must also deal with those traits in others. Having returned from an amazing jaunt across Spain, I was inspired to share these examples of love and adventure with those around me, but what I learned quickly is not everyone is receptive. In fact, many are either unable or incapable of understanding other perspectives.

I have learned through my own travels and numerous hobbies that the more experience a person has, the more they can relate to the world around them and the easier it is to find things in common with others. So naturally, people become more passionate about the world and understanding of other people with experience. People who have traveled the world or who take on diverse hobbies can relate to my story and don't judge me the way those with more limited perspectives do. I found after the Camino that I relate best to those who have ventured well beyond their front yard in exploration and those who seek more from their daily lives. But the truth is, many people refuse to strive outside of their comfort zone. These people are unable to understand what I've been through and where I am now. I have learned that people who thrive on the worst examples of humanity are deprived of joy, deprived of experience, and if you're not careful, they can very quickly suck you into their fictitious world of doom and gloom.

One example of the crippling effects of fear driven people occurred shortly after I returned from the Camino and was talking with a woman about my trip. Another man who I had seen before but had never spoken to walked in and said, "Theresa! You're back. I thought you were kidnapped." His comment confused me; it wasn't just what he said, but the way he said it. Almost in a mean, joking sort of way. At first, I thought perhaps he had heard about the American woman who went missing on the Camino just a month or two before I left for Spain. At that time, she hadn't been found, and pilgrims were subjected to all kinds of rumors about her disappearance (which I mentioned a few times in *Sunrise in Spain).* But I knew this man hadn't followed my blog, so I didn't understand his reference point.

He then explained that he has a three-year-old daughter, and that he was "going to make her watch all those movies like *Taken*", and was going to teach *his* daughter that "if she is stupid and acts like a whore, she's going to get raped and murdered." I felt myself go flush with rage and fear. Oh, the aggression, the anger, the hatred this man was spitting at me! All I could say was "…Wow." I could tell he was suddenly uncomfortable, and he responded with, "Oh, I'm terrified!" This was his way of offering up a justification for his atrocious perspective on life and women. The other woman chimed in with, "Well, we live in a very very dangerous world. Just the other day I heard the story about…" They began sharing the most horrendous stories. Here I was, filled with life and passion, talking about a spiritual pilgrimage, and somehow, they translated that into my being irresponsible and therefore deserving of any bad thing that could or may happen to me. To be so stricken with fear that they could not even hear my examples of how the whole world is not as horrible as they imagine was heartbreaking. I made an about face and walked right out of the room without another word, without participating in their rants. The woman caught herself and called out to me, "I really hope you had a great time, Theresa," but I was already headed outside.

I was enraged and scared by the man's aggression. It also made the feminist in me weep. How do I live in a world where people believe a woman deserves to be treated with such brutality for any reason whatsoever? This man is going to teach his daughter to be afraid of everything, to blame herself for every bad thing that happens to her, to reject exploration and adventure, and to not strive to be the most amazing human being she can. My heart broke, for that little girl, for myself, and for every woman who's ever been stuffed into a tiny box.

I climbed into my car and called Brian. I wasn't in tears but I was quite shaken and could feel my high blood pressure soak my cheeks with red heat. It would take me days to get over the verbal assault. When I explained what happened, Brian said, "Theresa, people aren't going to understand you anymore. All they do is watch TV, listen to politicians, and fill their heads with crap. They won't hear what you say, and you're going to have to work much harder now to find people who can relate to you." He encouraged me to seek connections with people who have had adventures, those who aren't so afraid of the world or of themselves, those who don't thrive on fear.

The painful truth is there are a disturbingly large number of people (even women who are adventurers themselves) who believe if a woman has the audacity to see the world (especially alone), she deserves whatever horrible thing that comes her way. I had heard this sentiment numerous times over the years both in general and directed at me specifically, but this was the harshest example. I violently reject everything these people think. Every human being has the right to explore this world however they deem appropriate. Yes, educate yourself, take precautions, be vigilant and aware, do your research, but *don't* let fear mongers and hateful people make you think you don't deserve to live your life to the fullest.

I want to be very clear that I am acutely aware of the world I live in and I would never say we're always safe, especially to women. As a four-and-a-half-foot tall woman, I have frequently been mistaken for a victim and have experienced some of life's harshest cruelties. So, I'm under no illusion that the world is full of rainbows and puppy dogs. That said, I have learned how to decipher between realistic risks versus irrational fear.

Fear mongers and small-minded people are not only focused on whether or not a traveler is a woman. Their negativity is far reaching and encompasses anything beyond what they're accustomed to. After giving over 30 talks around New England, a local television station heard a lot about my speaking engagements and contacted me for an interview. The interviewer said she would read my book ahead of time so she would be prepared. I was thrilled to be given an in-depth interview with someone who had a thorough understanding of my trip. This was a fantastic opportunity to further educate people and inspire them to seek out their own passion and adventures. However, when I arrived for the interview, I was confronted with resistance and hostility. The woman had not read my book and was less than interested in the topic.

Throughout the interview, I remained positive and tried to talk about all the gifts of long-distance hiking and traveling in general. But the interviewer was unable to hear my words and interrupted me frequently to interject her perspective on a subject she knew nothing about. She repeatedly asked me questions about my safety and well-being. "But what if you needed a doctor? Do they have doctors there? What if you got hurt? How do you go to the bathroom? Did you have to see naked men in the shared bathrooms?" All reasonable questions I'd become accustomed to addressing. But each of my answers were reciprocated with criticism. "This sounds like pure hell to me. What would possess you to do something like this? This sounds worse than joining the Marines. I can't believe your husband let you go alone."

I continued to defend the Camino's positive spirit but was always met with opposition from someone who has clearly never felt the need to challenge her views and stereotypes. She suggested the only reason I embarked on this adventure was because I was too young to know better, and when the interview ended, she said to me in a cold snarky tone, "Try to live to 40" suggesting I was taking unreasonable risks that would kill me. In case you're just chiming in, let me make it clear: I was in SPAIN! On a religious trail! I wasn't walking through a demilitarized zone in a third world country (which, by the way, many people have done without challenges). But it didn't matter. All this woman heard was that I had traveled beyond her small bubble, and for that she resented me and took every opportunity to make me feel as though I had done something wrong. I remained polite but afterwards asked for my interview not to be shared on the station's website. I could tell the woman thought I was overreacting and acting like a crazy lady, and perhaps I was, but I didn't care. I didn't want to be associated with people like her.

Brian too had to deal with negative people when he was preparing for his thru-hike, although people were less concerned with his safety and focused more on insulting him as a man. He was asked on more than one occasion, "When are you going to grow up?" As if somehow growing up was synonymous with never enjoying life again. Brian was genuinely disturbed that people thought so lowly of him, but obviously it wasn't enough to deter him. He asked me numerous times before he left if I was ok with him hiking while I stayed home and of course I was. What others didn't see was the hours, days, weeks, and months the two of us spent together planning to ensure I could maintain our life at home while he was gone.

Since my Camino and the subsequent interactions I've had with fearful angry people, I no longer taint my perspective with irrational fear. This means I don't watch dark entertainment, including movies, TV shows, and mainstream "news" outlets whose sole purpose is to incite terror and anger. These fear-ridden resources pollute our minds, distort our perspective, and stifle our creativity and sense of adventure to a degree most of us are completely unaware of.

The important lesson I took from all of this is to measure risk realistically and not to be deterred by the overwhelming negative stimuli we regularly encounter otherwise you could miss out on the very best experiences of your life.

Applying Lessons to Surviving a Pandemic

I never in a million years could have predicted this, but somehow Brian and I have managed to use lessons we learned from our long-distance hikes to help us survive the COVID-19 pandemic.

I recognize that Brian and I are extremely fortunate and privileged individuals. We have good jobs, a clean and safe place to live, and excellent healthcare. These are basic human needs that we have been blessed with, and without them none of these lessons would have made much of a difference. Many have had a far more difficult time and for others, this entire ordeal has been downright traumatic and life-changing on its own. In addition to the virus, our nation is also plagued by an equality toxic pandemic of social injustice, systemic racism, and political unrest. For many of us, the two crises are more than one could bear.

When I was initially told I would have to work from home for many months and that I should avoid all social situations, I quickly began to feel that helplessness, hopelessness, and emptiness that I felt after returning from the Camino. But this time I felt I had the tools and know-how to tackle my struggles head on. By the second week of being home, without full confidence, I revisited my lessons from long-distance hiking and began building a plan for the next few months.

First, I knew staying connected would be important. Fortunately for me, my friends were equally interested in staying in touch, so I set up video chats with different groups of friends. Sometimes we would work out together, sometimes we'd sit quietly in our grief, and sometimes we would drink ourselves silly. Either way I considered it quality time. Eventually, I discovered that in a way, the pandemic inadvertently closed the geographic gap as I began engaging with friends from other parts of the world more regularly and wondered why I didn't make more of an effort before the deadly pandemic.

Next, I knew I'd have to stay physically active to keep from collapsing into a depression. I pulled out my old P90X DVDs, which is a fairly hardcore workout program. I also increased my aerial training and was grateful I had equipment at home, since all the studios were closed.

Still, I wasn't sure how to manage that nagging uncertainty for the future. I had to frequently remind myself that every day that I woke up on the Camino, I had no idea where I would end up that night. I had never been to my final destination, so it was nothing more to me than a dot on the map. Yet, I distinctly recall writing in my journal one day, "Everything is going to be ok. You might not know how or even when. But everything will be ok." I also recalled the importance of being present when your destination is not in view. I'd put my head down, focus on my breathing, and just keep moving forward.

I thought of surviving the pandemic in the same way. I took it one day at a time. Some days were good and some days were bad though, I didn't fully understand why because my daily activities were essentially the same every single day. Over time though, the good days began to outweigh the bad days as I focused on small goals.

With all other aspects of my life on hold, I was able to focus solely on my mind and body. Brian and I immediately increased our time outside and time being physically active. It was only 42 degrees and there was still snow on the ground when we were biking through the woods, as best we could considering the conditions. In the beginning, I never once felt compelled to bike in the cold. It was never something I wanted to do and never once did I jump out of bed like "let's do this!" So, Brian and I had to push each other out the door every single day. As it began to warm up a bit, we teamed up with our neighbors and built a tiny bike path in the woods behind our houses. The path was only about a half mile that winded and bent all over itself, but it was the perfect outdoor retreat we needed and I took walks through the woods between work meetings. My tiny goals kept me focused and gave me a reason to get up in the morning. I tracked my good habits in a journal and it became a fun experiment to see how my mind and body responded to my actions. I paid careful attention to what made me feel energized and strong and what made me feel toxic and downright gross. I could see a gradual but obvious progression in my physical activity and I learned which foods my body responded best to. I discovered I needed additional vitamins and supplements to maintain my new active lifestyle. Eventually, with the excessive physical activity and a nutrient rich diet, my body became a finely tuned machine and my mind was just as strong. I dropped 15 pounds and my attention was unwavering. I knew this state of being was temporary and would only last as long as I could maintain that level of dedication, but that was ok. The point was, I had something with a positive outcome to keep me motivated through such challenging times. Training for my pole sport competition made me razor focused, ridiculously healthy, and insanely happy. And all that hard work, dedication, and self-discipline paid off because in November of 2020, I won the gold medal in my very first pole sport competition! I was filled with pride and gratitude.

I also learned it was ever important to eliminate the negative influences and all the hateful talk on social media. People are exceptionally scared, angry, and confused during this time in history,

I found myself (and everyone I knew) to be very sensitive to the negativity. As I watched others slowly unravel over the dumpster fires on social media and felt myself doing the same, I heavily restricted my own access and only received what I considered an adequate dose of statistics from specific sources to keep myself informed of the pandemic. The longer I refrain from participating in the distaste I could not control, the better I feel and the easier it is to cope with the things that really mattered, like being available for friends and colleagues who found themselves more seriously impacted.

The pandemic stretched on long beyond any of us could have imagined so every few months, I have to reassess how I am doing and find additional motivation to continue for a few more months. It is continuous work and I work hard to be kind to myself. As the realization that the pandemic will drag on even longer, I have to deal with the grief of lost opportunities. It takes me a couple of weeks to mourn what could have been and to say goodbye to the upcoming season before I can pick myself back up and carry on. I remember to be compassionate and wait patiently during these times, not fighting or denying the process and recognizing that these are unprecedented times and none of us are handling it like Rockstars.

While I feel my return from the Camino was difficult and painful, the lessons attained through those experiences have prepared me for events I never could have imagined. I don't know what the future holds for myself or for the world as a whole. But I know now that whatever happens, I'm going to do my very best to face things head on, having the tools I need to survive.

Was it Worth It?

So, here's the big question. Was hiking the Camino worth it? Of course, I had an amazing time while in Europe, but was that mere 5.2 weeks of my entire life worth the years of struggling after? I asked myself this nearly every day for the longest time. My knee-jerk reaction was to say "Yes, of course it was worth it!" But secretly there were many days I regretted every minute of it. I was angry at myself for deviating outside of my comfort zone and unwilling to forgive myself for being so naive. Perhaps ignorance really is bliss. Perhaps I would have been better off plodding along, thinking the life I was living was enough. Perhaps it would have been better to not have to go through the painful process of reevaluating my existence. I regretted putting myself in a situation that would ultimately require me to reconsider my entire life, that would force me to see the world differently, and sometimes uncomfortably, to make me crave more out of life, out of my relationships, out of myself. Had it not been for the Camino, I may have never experienced a period in my life where I felt so depressed, disoriented, and alone that sometimes it was difficult to breathe.

But that phase has passed, and I am on to a new one. Now, as I stand here more focused, with purpose, self-awareness, and passion for life, I can tell you absolutely, 100%, and a thousand times a day, YES! This completely unexpected life-changing adventure has helped shape the person I have become and the life I choose to live. I would not trade anyone's life with my own and I do not regret the tough lessons I had to work through. I love my Camino with all my heart and I love every gift it has bestowed onto me. One beautiful and poetic thought that always occurred to me, even when I regretted it, was either way I can never go back. I will never be the same. There are two parts of my life: one before the Camino, and the one following it.

Yes, there were many difficult times but every one of those endeavors have made me the woman I am today. I am not only the woman I want to be and living a life that feels truly my own but I am my own superhero. As for my life, rather than allowing it to be a meandering route of unconscious events, I am aware, I am focused, I am driven. I can see my path before me and I know how to reach my whole life goals. God Bless the Camino!

Parting Thoughts for Those Considering an Adventure

So, my lovely dreamers, adventurers, and doers. I will leave you with a few parting thoughts. If you're considering an adventure of your own, first and foremost know that I'm your number one supporter and you can always reach out to me if you need a cheerleader in your corner (or a swift kick in the keister).

When you return from your adventure, please keep a few things in mind as you transition back to reality. If your adventure includes long periods of time outdoors, know that a physical adjustment must be made from being outside all day every day, when your endorphins are pumping and dopamine levels are thriving. The return to a sedentary life can be physically and mentally painful. You can minimize these effects by finding ways to stay physically active and forcing yourself to spend time outside every day. Brian and I have learned that it's critical to our well-being post long-distance hiking to maintain a balance in our lives, properly managing modern day conveniences and comforts with adequate exposure to mother nature. But this is the beauty of adventure. There is no point in having a life-changing experience if it doesn't force you to better yourself and your life. Therefore, the work you do following your journey is just as important, if not more, than the journey itself.

To survive a possible harsh return to reality, and to fully honor the amazing benefits of a life-changing adventure, it will be paramount that you consciously incorporate the positive lessons into your life wherever possible. Those who don't bring those lessons to the forefront of their life struggle immensely. Brian and I must continuously work to honor our life altering gifts. He needs to be out in nature on a regular basis, and I need to travel regularly to new places. Once we identified these things as important to our well-being, we became much happier and content with our lives. The truth is most of us are living lives that are not meant for us. Modern life does not suit humans well. Sure, our creature comforts make us feel good temporarily, but the hustle and bustle of our lives leaves many of us depressed and anxious. Millions suffer but it's exacerbated in those of us who have been fortunate enough to experience a different and more meaningful way of living.

If you haven't had a major experience like this, you may have a loved one who has. Try to be patient with them. Talk with them. Ask them what's different now and find things in common with this new person. Respect that perhaps their needs have shifted. Talk openly about this.

If you're the one who has experienced this, work hard to understand the underlying changes you've experienced and respect the process. Understand that your answers may not come quickly. Give yourself time to readjust. How can you best assimilate to your previous life, and where do you need to make some changes? Don't expect to do this on your own. The process can be painful and you could benefit greatly from the help of others. Take comfort in speaking with those who have been through other changes and have already readjusted. You may take comfort in those who are equally struggling to adjust, but they may not be in the best position to provide the wisdom you seek. Find out what worked for others. Don't be shy about getting a therapist. Having a third-party perspective can be extremely helpful as they walk you through some of the most important questions you'll ever ask yourself. Be patient and kind with yourself, and above all, know that you have been given the amazing gift of a new perspective on life that can better your time here on earth, if you let it!

Acknowledgements

Thank you to my dear friends who not only provided the encouragement I needed to carry onward with my story but also gave me some darn good stories to talk about!

Thank you to Merry Lynne Rini and Jennifer Kingsburg for providing feedback on early drafts of this book.

Thank you to my friend Kolleen Carney Hoepfner who spent hours with me editing and combing through these pages.

Thank you to my friend and very talented author, Thomas J. Howley for bullying me into continuing to write whenever I wanted to give up on this project.

A huge thank you and hug to my Camino family for sharing one of the greatest times of my life with me: Ginger and Drennan Allen, Nikolai Jelgin, Melissa Christine, and Stephen McDaniel.

Thank you to my mother, Annette Gregg, who continues to be my number one fan.

And of course, my deepest gratitude goes to my amazing husband Brian for standing by my side through this fantastic life. You make my world spin, babe.

Portions of this book appeared in blog form: www.theresascamino.com

About the Author

THERESA FERSCH is a systems engineer by day, an aerialist by night, and an adventurer by accident. Following Theresa's first Camino, she converted her travel blog into a published book called *Sunrise in Spain* and began giving talks all over the east coast from small communities of two to crowds of 300. Theresa thoroughly enjoys coaching others and has recently decided to become a certified Life Coach, working with those who want to find balance in their life, who are struggling through transitions, and who are searching for their next great adventure. Today, Theresa and her husband Brian live happily in a small town in New Hampshire with their crazy husky, Bella. They spend as much time outdoors as possible and travel the world whenever given the opportunity.

Presenting at the Boston Public Library

Portuguese Camino 2019

15 mile day

Entering Spain October 14, 2019

Santiago de Compostela October 20, 2019

Being Silly

John Muir Trail 2017

The Cabin

New Hobbies